INSIDE
INTERMARRIAGE

INSIDE
INTERMARRIAGE

A Christian Partner's Journey
Raising a Jewish Family

Jim Keen

Foreword by Edmund Case

Behrman House
Springfield, New Jersey

To Bonnie, Gabrielle, and Molly,
whose love and laughter continually inspire me.

Versions of material in this book previously appeared in *The Guide to Jewish Interfaith Family Life: An Interfaithfamily.com Handbook* and at www.interfaithfamily.com

The publisher wishes to acknowledge the following "Other Voices" contributors:

Arlene Chernow: Chapters 1, 11
Karen Kushner: Chapter 3
Paula Brody: Chapters 4, 5, 6, 14, 17, 19
Howard Jaffee: Chapters 10, 15
Julie Webb: Chapters 13, 16
Ruth Goldberger: Chapter 20

Design by NeuStudio, Inc.

Behrman House, Inc.
11 Edison Place, Springfield, NJ 07081
www.behrmanhouse.com

ISBN 978-0-87441-986-3

Library of Congress Cataloging-in-Publication Data

Names: Keen, Jim, 1967- author.
Title: Inside intermarriage : a Christian partner's journey raising a Jewish
    family / Jim Keen.
Description: Springfield, New Jersey : Behrman House, [2017]
Identifiers: LCCN 2017013254 | ISBN 9780874419863 (pbk.)
Subjects: LCSH: Interfaith marriage. | Interfaith families. | Keen, Jim,
    1967- | Keen, Bonnie, 1967- | Jewish families--Religious life. | Child
    rearing--Religious aspects--Judaism.
Classification: LCC HQ1031 .K39 2017 | DDC 306.84/3--dc23 LC record
available at https://lccn.loc.gov/2017013254

Printed in the United States of America

CONTENTS

PART IV • CELEBRATING THE HOLIDAYS

PART V • MEETING MY OWN NEEDS

FOREWORD

By Edmund Case

When Jim Keen and his fiancée Bonnie were planning their wedding, her Jewish grandmother wasn't sure she would attend, because she disapproved of intermarriage. But she chose love, and she danced with Jim at the wedding, saying, "You're my grandson now." That story brought tears to my eyes, and it and others in this book might to yours. *Inside Intermarriage* is one of a kind: the warm, personal, light-hearted but very serious story of a Protestant man raising Jewish children together with his Jewish wife.

Interfaith couples like Jim and Bonnie who care about religious traditions face what I call "eternal" issues. Not in the sense that the issues can't be resolved, because they can be, as Jim's story vividly demonstrates. But all interfaith couples who want religion in their lives have to figure out how to relate to each other and their parents and families over religious traditions; they all have to resolve whether and how to celebrate holidays, to be spiritual together, to find community of like-minded people.

This book follows Jim's journey through all of those issues: from dating, falling in love, meeting the parents, deciding how children will be raised religiously, considering conversion, to getting married; from baby-welcoming ceremonies, to celebrating holidays, finding community, and meeting his own needs in a Jewish family. It's a deeply moving story, told with humor, and it's an important one.

Intermarriage is a significant phenomenon in the modern Jewish world. For many, it generates concern about how many children will be Jewish in the future. Jim Keen's example of one journey to Jewish continuity is reassuring. Interfaith couples who are interested in engaging in Jewish life and community can learn from Jim's story about how doing so can add meaning and value to their own lives.

Along his journey, Jim shares extremely helpful insights. For example, his and his wife's feelings and attitudes changed over time, with him moving from feeling different, "standing out," "not belonging," to feeling "part of." Another example: interfaith couples, no matter what path they follow, have to make a conscious effort to work out their religious traditions, which can lead to more thoughtful and deeper engagement. And another: interfaith couples aren't alone, and it's very helpful to connect and work through these issues with other couples.

Interfaith couples follow many paths, and Jim Keen doesn't say his is right for everyone. He continues to practice his own religion. Some partners in his position instead practice Judaism or even convert. Jim and his wife chose one religion for their children; some couples decide to raise their children in two religions, and many couples haven't decided, or haven't yet. Jim's clear advice is that there are solutions to the issues that interfaith relationships raise and that the key to resolving them is early and ongoing respectful communication. How Jim and his wife negotiated and communicated over many issues can guide you when faced with the same issues, no matter what path you may be considering.

Jim expresses deep gratitude for finding very warm and welcoming Jewish Community Center (JCC) preschool and synagogue communities and especially a rabbi by whom he felt genuinely embraced. It is essential that more interfaith couples experience that kind of welcome. Many Jews now have intermarried relatives, and many Jewish professionals are working with people in interfaith relationships. This book promotes better understanding not only of the eternal issues interfaith couples face, but also the perspective of the partner from another faith.

Jim Keen doesn't promote intermarriage, but he does recognize the positive effects, including an appreciation for tolerance and diversity. He writes that being in an interfaith relationship has broadened his perspective and enhanced not only his life, but also his parents' and in-laws' lives too. He still enjoys "belonging to [his] Scottish-American, Protestant group, but it's a warm feeling being able to see the world through Jewish eyes, as well." He also rightly recognizes his and his family's contribution to the Jewish community: "I am proud to say there are some Keens who happen to be Jewish. I love it."

Today, with so many Jews intermarrying, Jim Keen's perspective is more important and valuable than ever. Jim Keen and his family—on both sides—are heroes of Jewish life. They are role models for how parents from different faith backgrounds, together with all of the grandparents, can support the Jewish engagement of their children and grandchildren. They all deserve deep appreciation for this utmost gift, Jim especially for shedding light on the journey.

Edmund Case is the founder of InterfaithFamily and a writer, speaker, and consultant advocating for interfaith families' Jewish engagement.

InterfaithFamily is the premier resource supporting interfaith couples exploring Jewish life and inclusive Jewish communities. The nonprofit organization also offers education and training for clergy, organizational leaders, and other program providers, and provides comprehensive support in local communities.

PREFACE

Should I convert? Should I try to ask her to convert? If neither of us changes religions, can we get married? Who will officiate at the wedding? In what religion will we raise the kids? Wait, what will I tell my parents?

If you've picked up this book, chances are you've asked or heard these questions before. Being in an interfaith relationship can be scary. There's no point in denying it. It's purely frightening to love someone so much, yet to also have this nagging feeling that your union will implode because of your religious differences. Don't lose hope, though. It is possible for the situation to be successfully resolved.

You needn't feel that you and your loved one are the only castaways in this lifeboat at sea. Today, many people are in interfaith relationships and going through the same gut-wrenching emotions that you are. In fact, according to the Pew Research Center, more than half of Jews who take the plunge are jumping into an interfaith marriage.

I am a Christian dad helping to raise a Jewish family. My wife, Bonnie, is Jewish. We have decided to raise our children Jewish. And while our family dynamics are in perpetual motion, we have made many of the tough decisions. I have written this book with the hope that others can learn from our experience.

It's no secret that interfaith marriages are complicated, especially when both partners are connected to their own religious faiths and communities. While I do not encourage interfaith marriages, I recognize that they have become a fact of our society. When this happens, this book can help those couples by sharing our solutions—ones that give the children a clear Jewish identity, yet where both partners can feel comfortable.

Any family, no matter what the faiths of its individual members, can find our approach relevant. Interfaith homes come in all shapes and sizes. No two are alike. However, the foundations that will help them thrive are the same.

This book is not written solely for those readers who are inter-dating or intermarried. You may be a family member who is concerned for your son, daughter, sister, or brother who has entered into such a relationship. I have included material that is meant to be helpful to you as well. You may be asking questions like, "If my son marries outside our faith, will he be giving up who he is?" "If my sister's kids are raised Jewish, can I give them Christmas presents?" Perhaps you are a professional looking for a different perspective for the people you work with. Whatever your reason for reading this book, I hope you find it enlightening, entertaining, and helpful.

It all starts with dating—that is, if we can first overcome our basic differences. Then, before we know it, wedding plans emerge. And then, suddenly, the questions arise. What are we going to tell our parents? What kind of a ceremony are we going to have? Who is going to marry us? In what religion do we raise the children? How will we celebrate the holidays? Which ones? Yours or mine? Finally, how can each of us keep our own identity amongst all this give-and-take? It's not easy.

Read on. And, by all means, start talking with each other about the issues. There are workable solutions that will enable you to better enjoy your marriage, your family, and your life. Keep an eye open for the "Other Voices" sprinkled throughout the book. These experiences and tips offer insights from other interfaith couples. In addition, you'll also find a helpful discussion guide in the back. Use this as a tool to focus and promote meaningful conversations. I promise that this book will help answer your questions.

Part I
INTERFAITH DATING

CHAPTER 1

When We First Discover Our Religious and Cultural Differences

Do you remember when you saw your significant other for the first time? Your heart may have skipped a beat. You may have suddenly forgotten how to speak intelligibly. You may have even walked into a brick wall without noticing. Chances are, if you're Christian, you were only hoping that she'd agree to go out with you. Chances are, if you're Jewish, you were also hoping that she'd turn out to be Jewish too.

As an eighteen-year-old Protestant, making my way through my first year of college, I found out fairly quickly that I had no idea what I was getting into dating Jewish girls. My first clue came from just normal conversation, when I talked to some very nice girls whose conversation was sprinkled with Hebrew or Yiddish words that were unfamiliar to me.

Sometimes it felt like this: "Hi, my name is Jennifer, and last week at my sister's bat mitzvah, I sprained my ankle while dancing the hora, and that made me get *shmutz* all over my dress when I fell into a plate of chopped liver, which made my uncles mad, not because I made a mess, but because there actually was chopped liver, and the *simchah* was supposed to be *milchig.*"

My response: "Hi, my name is Jim. What's *shmutz*?"

Of course, nobody in real life actually talks like this, except for Jackie Mason, but it just emphasizes how foreign the culture was to me. Even a few Yiddish and Hebrew terms, sprinkled here and there, made me realize that I had a lot to learn.

(By the way, if you're like I was and don't understand a bunch of the Hebrew and Yiddish terms, look in the glossary at the back of the book for definitions. I'll try to explain them as they come up, but in the interest of fine literary flow, I may have to move on without an explanation.)

As a still-wet-behind-the-ears freshman, a conversation like that seemed to be a hint that the person was looking only for Jewish guys to date. However, looking back on it today, I can see that it was just a cultural difference that I did not yet understand. It was just like that first September when I was trying to figure out why a fourth of my dorm had gone home in the middle of the week. That's when my friend Jackie told me that it was the Jewish High Holiday of Rosh Hashanah. How would I know? It wasn't on *my* calendar.

Here I was, a freshman at the University of Michigan, whose large student body comes from all over the world and also has many Jewish students. Was I looking for Jewish women to date? No. But, my chances of meeting Jewish women were now proportionally higher than they were in high school.

While many of the Jewish women I met in college gave me what I felt was a subtle signal of "I'm Jewish, so back off" (of course, there couldn't have been any other reason they didn't want to go out with me), I knew that there were some who would take the attitude "What harm could it do if we take one day at a time?" By the second term of freshman year I met a woman named Bonnie. Actually, I chucked a Nerf football at her as she walked by my dorm room door. She threw the ball back at me, I whipped it back at her, she ran down the hall with it, and our relationship had begun.

For the next week, before I got up the nerve to ask her out, we would bump into each other in the cafeteria. I didn't know that she was Jewish. I actually thought that she might be Italian. It didn't really matter to me. She was cute, so my brain went into caveman mode. "Me big strong he-man. You woman. Must date."

It worked. I didn't make too big of a fool out of myself. Bonnie liked me. We went out to see a mindless movie, and she still liked me. I don't even think she told me she was Jewish until our second or third date. She laughed when I told her that I thought she might be Italian. She informed me that the two cultures have a lot in common: family gatherings that revolve around food, talking with your hands, etc.

Of course, once we had unceremoniously informed each other what our religions were, it didn't take long to learn more specifics. Bonnie had grown up in the Conservative movement of Judaism and still felt she belonged there. Some of her greatest memories were of getting together with her family for Passover and the High Holidays. Being away at college for the first time ever, she also deeply looked forward to going back home to keep alive those warm feelings of being with her family on special occasions. She didn't keep kosher at the time, but her identity was strongly Jewish—religiously and culturally.

My story was very different. My grandpa Keen had grown up a Presbyterian in Oklahoma. As a young man, his prairie church once reprimanded him for attending a dance. So by the time he moved to Michigan in 1925, to become the university's head wrestling coach and to attend law school, he had found a different church to call home. That's how I was baptized a

Methodist, instead of a Presbyterian. My family regularly went to services on Sundays, until we discovered hockey. My brother and I both played the sport. Unfortunately, and much to the chagrin of my mother, hockey games were scheduled on Sunday mornings.

Despite our decreasing attendance at Sunday school, my parents made sure that my brother, sister, and I never lost our faith in God. We always said our prayers at night and went to church as often as we could after the hockey season was over. By the time I entered college, I rarely went to services. Yet, even though I was out of touch with the church of my youth, I still believed in God. I still felt that Jesus was the Son of God. I still felt as Protestant as ever.

Despite being firmly rooted in our faith, my family had never stressed that there was only one true religion. As kids, we would ask my parents about Judaism or Islam. My dad always quoted my grandfather as saying, "Who's to say which religion is correct? There are many ways to explain God. All of them should be respected—except for those Lutherans." My grandpa Keen had a Mark Twain sense of humor.

Through Bonnie, I quickly discovered that many people from Jewish families have a strong desire to marry within their faith—more so than Christian families. A lot of this has to do with Jews being a minority. A lot of it has to do with the sheer tragedy of the Holocaust and how it highlighted the fragility of perpetuating the Jewish people. And much of it has to do with the fact that Judaism is both a culture and a belief system, whereas Christianity is primarily a belief system. You can be Jewish either religiously or culturally. You can be an atheist but still strongly identify with Jewish culture and history. You can't be a Christian and not believe in God. You then become just

American, or Scottish, or whatever your national heritage is.

It's not that Christians don't try to find other Christians to marry. Of course they do. Many Catholics may look for other Catholics to marry. Lutherans may look for other Lutherans. Greek Orthodox may seek other Greek Orthodox. What I didn't know, however, was that I was about to open Pandora's box. It never occurred to me that just dating could be a problem.

Whatever the backgrounds and circumstances, whatever the geographical origins, for some reason or another, Jews and Christians often find themselves falling in love. That's why you're reading this book. I hope I can straighten out some of this beautiful mess and show you that the relationship does not have to end. People *can* work around their religious and cultural differences and live to tell about it. You may also find your life exquisitely enhanced. How often do we get a chance to learn about, much less become part of another culture? Many people view that as a chance to broaden their minds, build understanding, and breed tolerance. Intentionally or not, Bonnie and I were about to go down that path. But it would not be without struggle.

OTHER VOICES

We tend to think that the way we did things in our homes growing up is *the* way to do them. This is true for any of us, whether Catholic, Lutheran, or Jewish.

Amanda's first Thanksgiving with Mark's family was difficult for her on many levels. Not only had she never been apart from her parents on Thanksgiving, she had also never met Mark's Jewish family before. She was horrified to find that Mark's family did not serve mashed potatoes as part of their Thanksgiving meal. The mashed potatoes became the symbol of how very different she and her boyfriend were at the time.

Amanda told Mark how much she missed her mother's potatoes, and he told her how much it meant to him that she was willing to spend this holiday with him. Not all issues will be as easy to resolve as the potatoes, but couples who often have problems tend to be those who are afraid to begin the process of exploration and discussion.

Couples need to be able find ways to explore many questions, such as what religious identity and community they want for their children, their individual relationships to God, and how much of what they cherish is cultural, and how much of it is religious. Having the courage to be open and clear about these issues will make couples realize that the fear of the discussion is much worse than the discussion itself.

CHAPTER 2

The Relationship Turns Serious: Now What?

I'm from Ann Arbor—the home of the University of Michigan. Had I socialized with Jewish girls before? Sure. I even dated a couple in high school. Ann Arbor has a very diverse population. However, I was totally clueless as to the cultural differences between Christians and Jews. The reason? Probably because in high school, the dating wasn't as serious. I wasn't looking for the love of my life. If the phrase "marrying outside the faith" came up with my high school girlfriends, I don't remember. I wasn't really paying attention. After all, we were only going to the movies.

In college, however, many relationships turn more serious. People consciously or unconsciously look for partners who will fit their notion (and their parents' notion) of the ideal spouse. Even though I didn't exactly fit the bill, being Protestant and all, my relationship with Bonnie had potential. In the back of my mind, I knew that she was Jewish and we might have problems. But at the moment, it didn't matter that we were of different religious and cultural backgrounds. We were having fun together and taking one day at a time.

As the semester continued, our relationship blossomed. Her grades went up, mine went down, and suddenly, we had summer break staring us in the face. Panicking, I asked, "What do we do? I'm from Ann Arbor; you're from Boston." It dawned on us that we would be apart for a few months. Nonetheless, we were still a couple and would not break up. The last few months had been wonderful. As different as our backgrounds were, we had so much in common and found it very easy to be together. Yes, we were getting serious.

Mike, my housemate, once asked me, "When did you know you were serious with Bonnie?" He had been dating someone for a few months and was starting to get that feeling.

"Do you remember your previous girlfriends," I asked, "how, when you would have an argument, that was the end of the dating? Well, you know you're serious when you have a fight about something, and all of a sudden, it matters to you. It hits you like a ton of bricks, 'I want to work this one out. I don't want to break up.' That's when you know you're serious."

So, Bonnie and I made plans to visit each other twice during the summer. In June, she would come to see me in Ann Arbor. In July, I would go to see her in Boston.

Bonnie's trip to see me at my parents' home was uneventful—great fun, but nothing unusual happened. After all, she had gotten to know my mom, dad, brother, sister, grandparents, and dog during the school year. They lived in the same town.

My parents had had a couple of small conversations with me about the difficulties that lay ahead by getting more serious with Bonnie. They never told me that they disapproved, though. They simply let me know that when people of two different religions get married, conflicts often arise, and solutions are hard to come by. Despite their concerns regarding my bold steps into this relationship, they already loved Bonnie. She was smart, she was funny, and she could dish it right back to my sarcastic brother, Tom. What wasn't to like?

My visit to Boston, to see Bonnie and meet her family, was a little different. It was great fun, once again, but quite eventful. She had warned me that meeting her dad might be a little different. "Why?" I asked.

"Because you're not Jewish."

"So?"

"*So*, when you're a Jewish girl, you grow up thinking that you're going to, someday, marry a 'nice Jewish boy.' My dad likes to perpetuate that idea. He was raised Orthodox. He has very traditional feelings about things like this."

This issue had come up over the last few months, but we had continued to brush it aside. They were the kind of conversations that we mentioned casually while lying around the dorm room studying—half concentrating on each other, half focusing on a political science midterm. We weren't *that* serious, were we? We weren't talking marriage—yet. So, the reality never hit home. Or, at least, we had not yet let it.

Bonnie and I knew that our relationship was becoming more and more meaningful every day. She had always thought that she'd marry within her religion, but now she wasn't so certain, even though we weren't even close to getting engaged.

As it happened, she introduced me to her father, stepmother, mother, and stepfather. Yes, I had not one, but two encounters of "meet the parents." I never had to hook up to a lie detector, but because Bonnie's parents were divorced and remarried, I had to go through that initial meeting twice. For all of Bonnie's parents, except her father, my being Christian didn't seem to be much of an issue. Or if it was, they never let it be known. They made me feel very welcome.

I knew that her dad would have been a lot more comfortable had I been Jewish. Nonetheless, we had a nice visit. He began to relax when he found out that my favorite movie was *Mary Poppins*—his favorite, as well. It turns out that we enjoyed a lot of the same films. This gave us something in common to focus our attentions. My breathing began to return to normal, too. All of us knew that we had a few more years of college before any talk of marriage would arise. Who knew what could happen in that time, so why force the issue now?

That was the first summer. But then came the second summer. We were still in love and determined not to break up. Then came the third summer, and I think our parents (all three sets of them) started to figure out that we were serious. This relationship quite possibly was going to lead to marriage. During this time, I saw her family in Boston, and sometimes they would come out to Ann Arbor for a campus visit. In addition, my parents saw us frequently at Michigan football, basketball, and hockey games. We all got along amicably, despite not having figured out the issue of religion.

Bonnie's father and I did have a couple of frank discussions where he told me his feelings of unease at the idea of a Protestant man marrying his daughter. He explained to me how the Jewish tradition was very important in his family. Intermarriage just wasn't done. He was concerned that Bonnie would lose her Jewish identity. He was also afraid that any future children of ours would not be Jewish. The Holocaust was still fresh in his mind, and it was particularly important to him that Jews preserve their numbers. If intermarriage became commonplace, the culture and religion would be in danger of dying off.

Although he said that he would love it if I converted, he

never pressured me and always made it clear that he liked me regardless of religion. The talks that he had with me were more about whether we had found a solution, rather than telling me what to do.

Because we were able to communicate openly, Bonnie and I understood what made her dad uncomfortable and why. She shared a lot of his feelings and, moreover, did not want to disappoint him. Although she had heard stories of children from Jewish families being disowned because of intermarriage, Bonnie didn't think it would get to that point in hers. Yet, she very much wanted her father's approval. We were also in love, and she did not want to give up on that. I knew that the conflicting feelings ate at her. Though I had not yet figured out how we would resolve our differences, my biggest fear was less about tradition, children, and conversion, and more about whether Bonnie would decide that getting married was simply too complicated. I also wanted—and needed—her dad's approval very much.

Bonnie and I began to talk more earnestly about possible solutions. Would I convert? I really did not want to. I knew the idea of her converting was not even worth bringing up. Could we just manage to maintain our respective religions in peaceful coexistence? Could we raise our children in both religions? Or should we pick one and raise them solely in that? I understood Bonnie's feelings about not wanting to give up her Jewish faith and identity. I did not want to give up my Protestant faith and identity, either. I wasn't sure how I'd feel about my children not believing that Jesus was the Son of God. Despite all this, we were both very committed to somehow making it work. But this sure was becoming a lot of mental anguish for something that started out as a simple date to see a Peewee Herman movie.

By the fourth summer, we had graduated from college. I proposed marriage that Memorial Day and admit that it was somewhat impulsive. I had an overwhelming feeling of love for this woman, and I didn't want to let her get away. We were out of school and heading toward our next stages in life. I was going into my family's business, and Bonnie was headed to law school. We had been dating for more than three years, and the time was right to make the commitment.

Perhaps somewhere in the back of my mind was the idea that engagement would force us to reconcile our issues a little faster, too, instead of just waiting for some solution to pop into our heads. However, we decided not to set a wedding date just yet. We both felt strongly that we couldn't say our nuptials until we had arrived at a resolution. We were now officially serious—diamond ring serious. Yet, we still had no clue as to how we would resolve our religious differences.

CHAPTER 3

When Did I Become a "Non-Jew"?

As my conversations with Bonnie kept ending with talk of still more talk, our relationship continued. Bonnie and I kept visiting with each other's families. We went to hockey games together, we went to dinner together, and we went to holiday gatherings in each other's family homes. She learned a lot about my family; I learned a lot about her family and Judaism. It seemed like there was never a moment when someone wouldn't take the opportunity to explain one aspect or another of the Jewish religion or culture to me.

"Every Friday night is Shabbat, or the Sabbath," my future father-in-law told me. "This is when we have a Friday night dinner. *Shabbes* is the most important of all Jewish holidays."

"Oh?" I answered innocently. "When is *Shabbes*?"

"Every Friday night."

"I thought Shabbat was on Friday."

"It is."

"What's the difference between Shabbat and *Shabbes*?"

Seeing my confusion, he answered, "Nothing. They're the same thing. *Shabbat* is the Hebrew word for the Sabbath; *Shabbes* is the Yiddish."

"What's the difference between Hebrew and Yiddish?"

"*Oy.*"

My education was just beginning. One summer evening, Bonnie's dad and I were talking amicably about Jewish holidays. Taking a twisted ram's horn down from the shelf of his Boston living room, he asked me if I knew the name of this common Jewish symbol. For some reason, I remembered the word "chauffer" from watching it blown during a Rosh Hashanah service that I attended with Bonnie. "Shofar," he corrected me. Then he asked me if I could blow it. Thank goodness I used to play trumpet in my junior high band. I think I grew three inches right in front of him at that moment.

Bonnie's other parents also liked to teach me about Judaism and its culture. Her stepfather and I discussed Israeli politics together (something that had never interested me before). He also enjoyed teaching me expressions in Yiddish (in which he is fluent). Her mother and grandparents fed me copious amounts of various Jewish foods. I learned what a kugel was and the proper way to pronounce it. And, Bonnie's stepmother taught me a lot about women in Jewish history—something I am grateful to pass on to my daughters today.

This learning experience was all very nice. However, while everyone was trying to accommodate me, I couldn't help but feel a little conspicuous. I knew that Bonnie's family went through the pains of teaching me because they were trying to include me. In their efforts to help me fit in, though, I was starting to feel even more like an outsider.

Suddenly, I was a "non-Jew." It's a crazy feeling discovering you're a non-something. You usually walk through life thinking of yourself as a something, but never the opposite of something. I can safely say that, on my census form, I've never put down "non-female" or "non-dependent" or "non-sixty-five-year-old."

This feeling began to grow during the Passover seders,

Thanksgivings, and other get-togethers with her parents and extended family. The first time we gathered together with her aunt, uncle, and cousins was a big Thanksgiving weekend on Long Island. Her cousin James had just gotten married. His wife Janice was also from the area, and her parents came to the dinner, too.

This was also the first chance the family had to view the wedding video together. Here it was, my first night with everyone (the whole *mishpachah*), and we sat down in front of the TV. The wedding looked like a lot of fun. I saw James break a glass, I saw people dancing in a circle, and I saw lots of food.

I also got to hear Uncle Sidney's toast. Part of it went, "Roses are red, violets are blueish. We all love Janice, and thank God she's Jewish." Everyone in the video laughed uproariously. Those sitting in the living room started to chuckle, then stopped as they remembered that I was there.

Cousin Ken leaned over to me as the video played on and asked if it had made me feel uncomfortable. "Uncomfortable? Heck no," I replied. "That was hilarious." And it was. I can recognize good humor when I see it. It takes a lot more than that to offend me. I still felt different from everyone else. It took a few years for that feeling to dissipate. I didn't feel annoyed or hurt—just different and maybe a little lost.

At the same time that I was experiencing feeling like an outsider, spending time with Bonnie's family was also making me want to become a part of her family—from her parents to her aunts, uncles, and cousins. Despite the differences, I liked them. I wanted to fit in.

Later that night, as we all went to bed in her uncle's house, the lights had no sooner turned off when somebody accidentally (and loudly) banged into a big brass ship's bell in the kitchen.

"Time to get up!" roared Uncle Sid. I could hear everyone laughing from inside his or her room. A bell also went off in my head. Her family was not so different from mine. We enjoyed good conversation and funny jokes, and we had a lot of the same personalities. Looking back on that weekend, it was actually the beginning of my sense of belonging, of losing the feeling of being a non-Jew. I began to see that though I wasn't Jewish, I could still fit into the family as myself. Despite our differences, we had things in common.

That incident was the start of my feeling like I didn't want to stick out. I began wanting to discover more about Judaism. Over time, and through many Jewish events, I took the opportunity to learn. I also became more comfortable in my new Jewish surroundings. Each year, the feeling of standing out lessened.

That's the thing about Bonnie's family. They went out of their way, right from the start, to make me feel a part of the group. Whenever something Jewish came up, like a ritual or an expression, they took time to explain it to me. They translated Hebrew blessings into English for me. On Passover, they told me the significance of each object on the seder plate. It took a few years, but I really began to feel comfortable with saying the blessings, with performing the different holiday rituals, and with knowing that her family was welcoming me in. As time went on, they began to think of me as part of the landscape. I was a reality, and they accepted me. Knowing this made me want to participate more.

I think I felt like a non-Jew because I was learning a whole new culture all at once. It's like being the new kid in school, or showing up late for a meeting and having everyone fill you in on the project. It takes a while for you to feel truly involved.

There were other issues bothering me at the time, too. I

couldn't help but wonder, by learning and participating in so much Jewish ritual and culture, if I was starting to lose my Christian identity. Was Jesus okay with this? It may sound funny, but how was I to know? I knew that I was still Christian. I still had my faith. But sometimes, when I was feeling particularly guilty that I might be abandoning my upbringing, I made sure to get to church that Sunday. Bonnie once asked me why I always wanted to head to church right after the High Holidays. It was at that moment that I realized I needed to relax. I was a Protestant all year round. I didn't have to get a dose of Christianity every time we celebrated something Jewish. I could still learn about Bonnie's faith and culture without undermining my own. How else were we to come together as boyfriend and girlfriend? As husband and wife?

When Bonnie and I were dating, she taught me several terms for non-Jews. I'm told that some of these may be offensive in certain contexts, so be careful how and when you use them.

"Gentile" is a word that most non-Jews have heard. It basically refers to anyone who isn't Jewish.

The Yiddish word for "gentile" is *goy.* You may hear this word when Cousin Rachel brings her non-Jewish boyfriend, Chris, to a wedding. Aunt Silvie will say, "Oy, he's a *goy.*" The plural of this word is *goyim,* which means "nations" in Hebrew. It comes from the sense of "people of other nations." As a boy, Colin Powell was a *Shabbes goy.* That is a non-Jew who is hired by Jews to do various tasks around the synagogue or a Jewish home on Shabbat (the Jewish Sabbath)—jobs like lighting the fire that are technically considered work and therefore forbidden on that day. Legend has it that Powell learned to speak fluent Yiddish by doing this, a skill that impressed his Israeli counterpart at their first meeting when he was secretary of state.

Moving toward the less refined of terms, *shiksa* refers to a non-Jewish woman. It is often used to refer to the archetypical blonde, non-Jewish woman. Today, its use is more general. It is important to note, however, that though this word is used casually in everyday conversation, its origins are quite unpleasant. It actually comes from the Hebrew word used in the Bible to mean "abomination."

One last relevant expression is "member of the Tribe." No, I'm not talking about the Cleveland Indians. The Tribe, in this case, is the Jewish people. My friend Matt invited me to a fundraiser for the Holocaust Memorial in Detroit. During dinner, one of his Jewish friends said to me, "You're not a member of the Tribe, are you?" The comment was not one designed to exclude or ostracize me. In fact, it was said during the friendly conversation we were having about Michigan football. How it fit into that exchange, I'll never remember. Sometimes this term is shortened to M.O.T.

I can see where use of these words and phrases can make a non-Jew feel out of place, particularly around a group of strangers with whom you're trying to fit in. As I found out, even some Jews are not comfortable with any of these names.

Our society craves labels. We love to know how to identify and classify objects, places, and people. In the world of interfaith marriage and the Jewish community, we habitually refer to the people in the relationship as the "Jew" and the "non-Jew." Even relatives of the couple get labels—for example, the "Jewish grandparents" and the "non-Jewish grandparents." Perhaps because classifying people can hint at some sort of hierarchy, there is a movement among synagogues and outreach professionals to do away with the term "non-Jew."

Although I am used to others referring to me by this moniker,

I support the idea of changing it. The question is, to what? What would be a better term than "non-Jew"? I'm a Protestant; you could always just call me that. However, that doesn't fix the problem of general terminology when referring to a group of people of unknown background. I know of some outreach professionals who call the non-Jew the "person of other-faith background." Accurate, but it's a mouthful.

We already have a couple of words for the "person who didn't grow up complaining about going to Hebrew school." There is the Hebrew and Yiddish word *goy*. The problem with *goy* is that it's considered derogatory. Then, there's the word "gentile." Nothing mean about it, except that it's just so old-fashioned and musty.

It's clear that we need something new. How about "Jewish supporter," as in someone who supports the Jewish spouse? Nah, it sounds too much like "athletic supporter." How about "friend of the Tribe"? We already have "members." The abbreviation could be F.O.T. This name is too broad, I think. The problem is that it could also simply refer to someone who supports Israel but is not in a relationship with a Jewish partner.

What about affiliated, adjunct, cohort, consort, federated, or associate? According to *Roget's Thesaurus*, these words suggest one who is united in a relationship. "Associate-Jewish partner?" Nope. Too reminiscent of a lawyer's title. "Did you hear about Bob? He just made associate-Jewish partner!"

Sadly, I don't think that there's an existing word in English to describe what we are looking for. According to Bill Bryson, William Shakespeare invented a few thousand words of his own including "*lonely, leapfrog, zany, well-read,* and countless others—including *countless*!"

Now I couldn't soliloquize my way out of a wet paper bag, but I think a new word is in order here, because with a rate of about

50 percent, intermarriage is very common in America. We used to get many of our words from French, Latin, and Greek. As our language stateside continually evolves, now we are getting many of our new words from Spanish: salsa, cafeteria, macho, El Niño, ay caramba!

In Spanish, "other faith" is *otra fe*. Maybe we can create a new word: "otrafay" (it's more phonetic). It is only one word, has three syllables, and can be used in many situations: the Jewish spouse and the otrafay spouse; the Jew and the otrafay; the Jewish grandparents and the otrafay grandparents. New. Succinct. Accurate.

Use this word at your next dinner party or during the after-service *oneg*. You'll be on the cutting edge. Sure, it may take a while for "otrafay" to catch on, but that's fine. I wonder how long it took English kids to call jumping over one another "leapfrog"?

No matter what term we use though, feelings of not belonging are natural and expected. On Shabbat, I was constantly afraid of drinking the wine at the wrong moment during the Kiddush, the blessing over the wine. I was nervous that I would break off too big of a piece of challah during Hamotzi, the blessing over the bread. On a couple of occasions, I nearly blew out the Shabbat candles instead of letting them burn completely down. Of course, my mind ran away with what the punishment might be for such an offense. I imagined the family having to read the entire Torah in one breath, while fasting for forty days.

The first time I went to temple with Bonnie and her parents, I was sure I would be "outed" right there in the synagogue, in the middle of the service. I thought the rabbi would look up and see me, the only one not reciting the prayer in Hebrew, and have me tossed out. I later found out that many Jews don't know the Hebrew, either. Turns out I *could* blend in after all.

Yet, I persevered. What made me want to keep learning—keep putting myself in situations of anxiety and potential ostracism? This was not the familiar, comfortable territory that I had grown up with. I guess it had to be love. There are simply some things worth getting sweaty palms over.

Before I make it sound too easy, not every member of every family will go out of his or her way to make you feel welcome. I consider my experience fortunate. However, there are family members for whom it takes a while to get comfortable with the idea that someone in the family is inter-dating or intermarrying. This may come in the form of avoidance, not being included in family functions, not attending one of your functions, or even outright, in-your-face confrontation. Just try to understand the source of their dissatisfaction before you pass judgment back on them. Some people may simply be close-minded. Some may be open-minded but unable to accept your relationship based on their religious beliefs. Some may not even care about your non-Jewishness. They just may not like you because you wouldn't eat their gefilte fish.

Whatever your experience, don't let the ups and downs take a toll on your relationship with your partner. Bonnie and I had a few heated discussions about unrelated matters but often found them to be incited by feelings of not fitting into the other's religious activities. Sometimes I didn't want to let myself enjoy the experience, scared that I might lose my own identity. Other times Bonnie wasn't comfortable with being a part of my Protestant culture or participating in my religious celebrations. One Christmas Eve, we were planning on attending the church service with my family. Bonnie and I had already established our game plan that she was only going to help me celebrate my holiday. But, all throughout the day, we found ourselves squabbling about everything in sight—the right thing to wear, the possibility that my mom might use Christmas wrapping paper on a gift for Bonnie, the dishes not washed. You name it; it became a point of contention that day. And, this was *after* we had been married for a couple years.

When we finally analyzed it, we were both a little nervous about the holiday and how we would *both* fit in. There would be Bonnie—a Jewish woman in a Protestant church. What should Bonnie do while there? There would be me—the Protestant guy with the Jewish wife. How do I act at church now? How do I participate without looking like I'm trying to make up for having gone to temple? How do I make Bonnie comfortable? Growing up as a minority and being overwhelmed by the Christmas marketing season, Bonnie had never felt that great about this holiday. In fact, it made her uneasy at times.

Once we were able to get to the heart of the issue and realize the root of our anxiety, we knew that things would be better. We both were trying to fit in. At least we would give the bickering a rest for a while. We were in this together and that was comforting.

It took a little time, but learning more about each other's religion was actually a lot of fun. We began to feel a sense of purpose and determination to research as much about our religions as possible. The more we were informed, the better our decisions would be. In addition to learning from each other and our families, we attended an introduction to Judaism class together and talked to an intermarriage counselor.

It also helped me to feel comfortable with being a non-Jew in her presence, in her family's presence, and while participating in Jewish activities. With my ever-growing knowledge of Judaism, I was able to know what to expect ahead of time.

Being a non-Jew involved with a Jew can bring about an overwhelming set of feelings. As I got more comfortable with the Jewishness of Bonnie and her family and friends, I found myself being able to move in and out of that group, depending on the situation. Now, on the Jewish holiday of Sukkot, I can feel that I'm part of the celebration. One day, I can build the sukkah, shake the *lulav* and *etrog.* The next day, I can turn around and go to church, feeling just as Protestant as ever. In the early days of our relationship, I couldn't do that. I would not allow myself to enjoy a Shabbat dinner or temple service because I was too afraid that I was doing a disservice to or losing sight of my own religion. However, as I continued to attend church and celebrate the Christian holidays with my family, I learned that I could do both. I could still be a Christian *and* help Bonnie enjoy her religion and family get-togethers. I had to try it to know that my Protestant faith wasn't going to disappear simply because I helped someone else experience her religion. I would still be able to spend the holidays with my family, and I would still be able to love Jesus. It may sound strange, but I would still be able to watch *A Charlie Brown Christmas* on TV. Time and experience showed me that Snoopy wasn't going anywhere.

OTHER VOICES

Bethany and Ben had been dating for two years, starting when they were both in the Peace Corps in Uganda, learning a language and a foreign culture. With all her skills in biculturalism, Bethany was expecting an easy time fitting in with Ben's family for the week of Passover. Ben told her that his family was not very observant of the laws of the holiday, and he was looking forward to showing off the bright, caring woman he loved very much. His family had spoken to Bethany on the phone and was excited and eager to meet her.

It was thus a huge shock to find his normally very secular family insisting on reading every page of the haggadah. Not only that, but his very fashionable, worldly grandparents were using Yiddish expressions and telling "in-jokes" that made Ben lose his appetite. Bethany had never before felt like a non-anything, but suddenly she was very aware of her non-Jewish status.

Bethany worked hard to follow the confusing progression of the Passover ritual and found it as difficult as her early days in Africa. Ben helped as much as he could but found he could not answer most of Bethany's questions. Later that evening, Ben realized that his family had reacted to Bethany's Christianity by overemphasizing their Jewishness. Bethany alternated between being angry and sad over what felt like a rejection by Ben's family and an indication of what might be a lifelong struggle with her future in-laws.

Through honest conversations over a period of time and a growing sense of mutual trust, these feelings were eventually dispelled. Though Ben's parents and Bethany grew to value, love, and respect one another, it was an awkward and confusing beginning that took patience and understanding on everyone's part to overcome.

CHAPTER 4

What Religion Would Our Children Be?

Bonnie and I had started to discuss the issues about our different religious backgrounds over that period of time leading up to our engagement. Bonnie's dad was still uncomfortable with the idea that I wasn't Jewish. On top of it all, her Orthodox grandmother, or *bubba*, as she called her, told Bonnie that she wished her well but couldn't attend our wedding. It was a matter of principle for her. Things like these get you talking about the details in a hurry.

Having members of her family not 100 percent behind her put a great strain on Bonnie. Sometimes she felt as though she were being forced to make a choice between her family and me. Of course, this put me under a lot of stress, too. Not only did I hate to see my fiancée go through this anguish, but also I worried that it would spell the end of our relationship. This was not going to happen. We both understood that we needed to find a solution.

How would we resolve our differences? We knew that we wanted to spend the rest of our lives together. But how could we if we couldn't figure out the religion question? I was comfortable with her being Jewish. She was fine with me being Protestant. We had explored the idea of one of us converting.

It wasn't simply a matter of "You convert"—"No, you convert."

Neither one of us felt right about asking the other to make such a profound change. We knew each other too well. We knew that our identities were important to us. And, although I was learning about Judaism, I still didn't know it well enough to say, "Hey, I like this a whole lot better than Christianity."

So, the conversations were more on the lines of "What if one of us were to take classes about the other's religion, then that person could decide . . . no that won't work. Forget I said it."

In the end, we decided that it was too much to ask of one of us. We were both fairly religious and rooted in our faiths. I knew other couples where one partner converted. It seemed, however, that the one who made the switch had never really felt at home in his or her original religion. For those couples, it was probably a good decision. But, we knew that we would never feel comfortable during our marriage if one of us left the faith and background that had meant so much to us.

Bonnie and I had to think about the real motivations behind conversion. A counselor we talked to and the books we read reinforced our decision. When someone converts, it should be for the right reasons. That person should feel that the change helps them become more of their true self. Our religious identities were tightly woven into the fabric of our families, to whom we were very close. Making a change in our religious identities would have to be an authentic choice for either of us.

We did not want to make such a drastic life change just to please each other or our parents. That would be the wrong reason and would likely lead to years of unresolved resentment. I knew that Bonnie's dad would be disappointed. But at the same time, I felt relief that Bonnie backed me up with her father. Conversion to Judaism simply wasn't going to happen. We would make it work another way.

That part was settled. Bonnie would continue to be Jewish; I would still be Protestant. We felt that we had reached an important milestone, but we were still nowhere close to solving the problem. Our discussion then started to center not on what religion we would have, but on what religion our kids would have. Children? (See Jim. See Jim's head spin.) We promised each other that we would have it ironed out before the wedding. This was a toughie. We certainly had our work cut out for us. Fortunately, we weren't alone. Our parents, even her dad, cared more that his daughter was marrying someone she loved, and someone who loved her, than that she marry a fellow Jew. Our parents came to realize that we made each other happy. They offered us not so much advice, but support. Meanwhile, Bonnie and I continued to talk and talk and talk and talk.

Simply being married to a person of a different faith was a tough issue, but certainly workable. Aside from the wedding day itself, the thought of just the two of us going through life wouldn't be so difficult. You celebrate your holidays; I'll celebrate mine. It could be a sort of "live and let live" attitude. However, this was not the kind of relationship we had envisioned having forever. We both, eventually, wanted children. There was the problem.

"I'm comfortable with you being Christian, but I would like the kids to be Jewish," Bonnie had said.

"I'm all right with you being Jewish, but I'm not sure how I'd feel if our children did not believe in Jesus as the Son of God," I replied. I had always been tolerant and respectful of other religions. But, suddenly, I wasn't so sure how I'd feel if my own children had a different set of beliefs.

Impasse reached.

This is where most interfaith couples realize the complexity of their situation. It's one thing to be tolerant and accepting of another person's religion, but it's a whole other world when you bring your children into the picture. These will be my offspring—my legacy—the ones who will carry our family name and traditions into the future. The possibility of raising your children in a religion that is not your own can be overwhelming. I also had to picture my role in raising my children in a different faith. Would I feel a part of the family? Would I know what to do?

Fortunately, even though we were in love, we didn't just jump into marriage without first working out this issue. We were engaged but knew that we couldn't get married until we had found a solution. Over the next two years, we talked about the dilemma constantly. We also read what few books there were on interfaith marriage. Unfortunately, there was no InterfaithFamily.com or books from any different points of view yet. We could have used such resources.

We weren't without assets, though. Bonnie's stepmom just happened to be a social worker who specialized in interfaith relationships. In this role, she helped us navigate many of the tough issues. We also sought the wisdom of our other parents. They also gave us sound advice based on common sense and life experience.

All of the input certainly helped. However, what worked best for us was the hours and hours of talking to each other and trying to figure out what our religion meant to each of us. Every once in a while, our conversations would get heated, but we never for a minute wanted to give up. We knew we had come too far and loved each other too much to let anything get in the way of our spending the rest of our lives together.

In many interfaith families, the partner who is less religious often offers to raise the children in the other spouse's faith. Our problem was that we were both pretty religious, had strong family ties, and had wonderful memories of celebrating the holidays with our respective families.

In the end, we decided to raise the kids Jewish partly because Bonnie would be moving away from her family in Boston to live with me in Ann Arbor, where I was born and raised. She felt that a lot of her Jewish identity was a direct result of being around her parents and cousins. Raising our kids Jewish would help her feel that she was still in a Jewish home. On the other hand, I would still be living in the same town as my Christian family. In addition, because Bonnie had come from a Conservative Jewish background, she had grown up believing that it was the mother's religion that determined the children's identity, since the greater Jewish community accepted matrilineal descent. Interestingly, today Bonnie considers herself a Reform Jew, and that particular issue is of less importance, since Reform Judaism considers children of either a Jewish mother or a Jewish father to be Jewish if they are deliberately raised as Jews.

A friend of mine recently asked me how I decided to give this "gift" to my wife. She wanted to know what factors made this the right choice. I had a hard time answering that one because nothing forced us to decide one way or the other. The only criteria was that we both had to be happy with the resolution. There is no right or wrong answer.

I had come to terms with my exact feelings on my religion. I was still Protestant, and I was secure in my identity. I had always been accepting of different religions and their beliefs. Here I was about to marry someone who did not share all of my viewpoints. I was fine with that. It dawned on me that if I were to love and respect this person with whom I was about to spend the rest of my life, I could certainly feel the same way toward my children. We would be one family. It no longer made sense to me that acceptance could apply only to one member. It somehow just *felt* right. Today, as we raise our two Jewish daughters, it still does.

OTHER VOICES

Talking about how couples will raise children in an interfaith relationship definitely puts their communication skills to the test—sharing what they need, and listening to what each partner needs and why. Negative family experiences, even a lack of family experiences, shape these needs deeply.

Marcia, who is Jewish, felt deeply tied to her Jewish identity but had very few memories of family religious experiences from her childhood. Marcia's mother had died when she was a young girl, and since then, her family no longer celebrated Jewish rituals. She wanted to give her children the fond family memories she had lost as a child.

Paul was raised Protestant in a family that had had many religious traditions—regular church attendance, Sunday dinners, wonderful holiday celebrations, and grace before meals. Paul remembered these family traditions with much fondness but felt he was no longer connected to the "faith" aspects of his religious upbringing.

When Paul and Marcia expressed their own needs for religious traditions in their family, they both felt a strong need to create shared family rituals. Paul wanted to commit to using religious rituals to bind their family together, creating the strong family memories for their children that he had had growing up. Paul felt he could raise his children within Judaism as long as they, as parents, re-created many shared family traditions he loved—including regular worship attendance, Shabbat dinners, joyous holidays, and blessing before meals. Paul wanted to give Marcia the gift of raising children in her Jewish faith because he realized that she had lost so much when her mother died. Marcia was tremendously appreciative of Paul's support, asking him for his help in creating these special family moments built around their commitment to raise children within Judaism. Because Paul and Marcia focused on what they needed for themselves religiously, rather than trying to imagine what their future children would need, they were able to feel good about the decisions they made regarding their children's religious upbringing.

CHAPTER 5

Telling My Parents We're Raising Jewish Kids

As a Protestant, I always assumed that one day I'd be taking my future kids to Sunday school. I also thought that I'd be teaching my future son to play baseball. But, as it turned out, I took my kids to shul (Yiddish for "school"—more specifically, the synagogue). It also happened that my kids are daughters, and I took them to ballet! Life throws you unexpected curveballs, and you deal with it. Now that I actually have a family of my own, I feel blessed to have two wonderful girls. The decision to raise them in the Jewish faith was not an easy one, but it's one I don't regret. What was equally hard was telling my parents.

Telling my in-laws was easy. After all, they're Jewish. Even though I did not convert, I think they felt fairly comfortable knowing that I would make every effort to help my wife teach the kids the Jewish faith and traditions. Telling *my* parents would be a different story. What on earth would I say? How would I broach the subject? What would their reaction be? Would they disapprove? Would they disown me?

Fortunately, my parents have always been loving and supportive, so I didn't think they would do anything rash.

However, these thoughts did go through my mind because this was alien territory for them as well. Many interfaith couples *do* face strong disapproval from their parents when the news is broken. We've all heard the stories, and we've read the books. We may even know someone who's had problems. That someone could have been me.

No matter how open your parents are, there are some talks you have to be well prepared for if you want them to go right. My wife and I went over and over our reasons for raising the kids Jewish: We wanted to raise them in one faith so as not to confuse them. Also, because their mother is Jewish and from a traditional Conservative background, they would be considered Jewish at the Conservative synagogue where Bonnie was then a member. However, we wanted to teach them about Christianity, my religion, to enrich their lives and give them an understanding of their heritage. They would still be allowed to "help" their Protestant grandparents and me celebrate Christmas and Easter. But, they would know that, bottom line, they are Jewish. Also, it would be really nice if my Protestant parents helped my children celebrate Jewish holidays like Shabbat, Sukkot, and Hanukkah.

This was great in theory, but how would it work when we actually told my parents face to face? (I want to emphasize "face to face." This is not something you want to do over the phone, if possible.) If they gave us any argument or grief, we had to be prepared to tell them that it was important to us that they respect our decision. In addition, we needed to say that we'd put a lot of thought into it, we felt it's best for the kids, and most of all, we really wanted them to be included in the raising of our children.

That last part is what really helps you over the hump. It's crucial to let your parents know that you still want them to help and be involved. You want them every bit as active as they would have been had you decided to raise the kids Christian. This lets them know that they are needed. Obviously, they won't know very much about the Jewish holidays and life-cycle events, but you can teach them. And in turn, they can participate. Just being there is important. The Protestant grandparents can come over for a Shabbat dinner. They can assist in putting up the sukkah. They can play dreidel for chocolate *gelt* (or in our family, jelly beans).

As it turns out, we had "the talk" one evening over dinner at my parents' house. It was a little nerve-racking trying to find a way to bring it up, but somehow we managed to find the courage. My mom was talking about Christmas stockings.

"Someday, when you two have kids, we have to remember to tell Aunt Ann to make them stockings," she said.

"Uh, well, Mom, Dad, we'd like to discuss that with you a little bit. You see, about Christmas . . ." They didn't say too much while we explained our plan—they just let us talk. However, when we got to the part about how much we hoped they would help us, they finally spoke.

"We'd love to help," they said.

Huh? You mean, that's it? No arguments? No grief? Of course, it wasn't that simple—it never is. They still had their questions to ask. For instance, they wanted to know what to do about Santa. And every once in a while, we have to tell them that "we prefer to do things such and such a way."

They may have had an inkling from our previous four years of dating and engagement that we'd choose this route. But they hadn't been through the details of it like my wife and I had. My mother was very concerned that our children might go around telling their Protestant cousins that there's no such thing as

Santa Claus. We in turn explained how our kids would help them celebrate the Christian holidays. We used an analogy of a birthday party. When you go to another person's birthday party, you are helping her celebrate *her* birthday. It isn't *your* birthday, but you can still have a piece of cake. You may also receive a goody bag to take home.

I also know that my mother, for a long time, felt a little uncertain when it came to how she should approach religion with the kids. She had admitted to me that she was uncomfortable talking about baby Jesus in the manger. She didn't quite know what we wanted her to say to our kids or even if it was appropriate to talk about Jesus in the first place. I reassured her that when explaining her Christianity, she may say anything that she normally believes. She should feel safe demonstrating her religion, in her own home, the way she has always practiced it. But, in order to not go overboard, I suggested that it wouldn't be appropriate to talk about it as if it were something our children should believe in, too. She gave me a look that said, "Well, duh." At that moment I knew it would be all right. She may have been a little disappointed that she was in this position. I'm sure she always had visions of teaching her grandkids the Bible stories that she taught me. And there are times when I can still tell that she wants to go all out with our kids at Christmastime. But, somehow, she manages to restrain herself. With our continued guidance, I think that she has adjusted fairly well, considering.

For my dad, his biggest worry was that in focusing on Judaism with my kids, somehow I would lose sight of my Protestant traditions and background. I'm sure that he would love me no matter what, but it's got to be hard on a parent to think that his child would turn his back on so many years of upbringing. I reassured him that this was something that I would not and could not ever forget. As he watches us raise our family today, I know he feels good about how we haven't neglected having our kids help me celebrate my holidays. This is evident in the fact that he and my mom really get into helping my family celebrate Jewish traditions. They gladly come to our annual Hanukkah party, they attend Shabbat dinners with us at the Jewish Community Center, and they even smothered their granddaughters with hugs and kisses on the day of their religious school consecrations and bat mitzvah celebrations. I think they would have been less cooperative if they weren't comfortable with our methods.

All in all, they were, and still are, supportive of us raising our kids Jewish. I don't know if it was the part about including them or the fact that they wouldn't have to share us with my in-laws on Christmas and Easter. But my wife and I are extremely lucky to have parents who are understanding and want to help.

I'm not naive enough to think that this is the norm. Many parents facing the idea of their child marrying someone of a different faith may have stronger feelings about seeing their grandchildren raised in a different culture and religion. It's important to recognize and respect your parents' concerns. They have preconceived notions about your children and their role in your children's lives, just as you do. Hopefully, over time, and with a lot of coaching and conversation, you can get to a point where your biggest problem is trying to keep your dad from eating all the coconut-flavored jelly beans at Hanukkah.

OTHER VOICES

Many couples avoid making a decision about the religious identity of their future children simply because they do not wish to hurt one set of parents. Soon after their engagement, Mandy and John decided to raise their future children within Judaism but then decided they would not tell John's Catholic parents, fearing that John's mother, a very devout Catholic, would be terribly disappointed. Mandy and John decided not to tell Mandy's parents either, even though Mandy felt her parents would be thrilled that their Judaism would be passed on to their grandchildren. If John's or Mandy's parents asked whether they had made a decision about the grandchildren, their game plan was to say, "We have not yet decided."

Their silence about the decision as their wedding day approached left both sets of parents wondering if their adult children cared enough about their religious traditions to pass a faith on to their future grandchildren. Without telling Mandy or John, their mothers talked with each other, sharing their mutual heartache and opting to confront their children with their shared concern that their grandchildren would have no religion.

When confronted, Mandy and John initially stuck with their "we have not yet decided" response. Finally, their tearful mothers shared their anxiety, with each mother saying that they would rather have their grandchildren raised in one faith tradition than no faith or no decision made about a faith. In shock, John and Mandy conferred with each other and told their parents that they had indeed made a decision to raise the children Jewish. John's parents were more relieved than disappointed, and Mandy's parents, happy that a decision had been made, felt empathetic with their Catholic in-laws.

In hindsight, John and Mandy wish they had let their parents in on their decision sooner rather than later. Both sets of parents now gather with Mandy and John to celebrate holidays. Mandy's Jewish parents have accompanied John and his family to midnight Mass on Christmas Eve and have come to John's extended family's Catholic life-cycle rituals, including baptisms on the birth of new cousins. Both mothers enjoy making lots of matzah balls together for the annual Passover seder, to which all of John's family is always invited.

Part II
NEGOTIATING LIFE-CYCLE EVENTS

CHAPTER 6

When Nothing Else Will Do, Have a "Jewish-ish" Wedding

After determining what religion our children would have, it was time to set our sights on the wedding itself. Planning any wedding can be tough. When you're planning an interfaith wedding, however, "tough" is just a starting point. In our case, we had the pleasure of appeasing the usual wishes of both of our families (which guests to invite, who should accompany whom down the aisle, seating charts, and so on), but on top of it all, Bonnie and I had to decide if we were going to have a Protestant ceremony or a Jewish one.

Looking back, the first issue we ran into was trying not to offend any member of either family. My parents had their own visions of how a proper wedding should take place. These were probably ideas that had been cooking in their heads for years. Basically, Protestant weddings are plain and simple. There is no Protestant culture that is an integral part of the ceremony or reception (unless you count the garter toss). You walk down the aisle, a minister marries the bride and groom, maybe a song or poem is included, you walk back up the aisle, and then there is a party afterward.

There are countless Jewish wedding traditions, however, many of which Bonnie's parents considered important. For instance, there's a chuppah under which the couple are married, the breaking of the glass, the blessing over the wine, the blessing over the challah, and dancing the hora. Bonnie and I had the task of trying to make sure nobody felt uncomfortable on our special day.

"*Our* special day." We almost forgot. Somewhere along the way, we remembered that it was important for us to make sure our day went the way *we* wanted it to go. Don't get me wrong. Our parents were very cooperative and had only our best interests at heart. But we were the only two people who could plan our wedding the way we wanted it to be.

Exactly what did we want? We started by making a list of all the things that were important to us. Bonnie had been to many of her cousins' Jewish weddings and was accustomed to seeing the traditional Jewish elements. She had always felt that these features would be there when she herself became a bride. These traditions were totally foreign to me and made me nervous that my side of the family would feel completely lost and neglected.

I never really thought much about weddings. I hadn't been to many weddings at all, let alone a Jewish wedding. There weren't any burning Protestant cultural elements that I just had to have. Although I'm of Scottish descent, I felt that kilts would be a little too much for her family to take.

But there was one thing about which we both felt strongly— we wanted to have God as part of our ceremony. After all, God is a big part of our lives. So would we have a minister marry us? What about a rabbi? Given our feelings about our faiths, either of those choices wouldn't be fair to one of us. Bonnie said that having a minister perform the ritual would make her feel that it was a Protestant wedding. Likewise, a rabbi would give the service an overly Jewish tone for me. Although we had decided that we would raise our children Jewish, we still couldn't have a Jewish wedding. For this, all our Jewish family and friends told us, you need both the bride and groom to be Jewish. It wasn't until later that I learned there are rabbis who will officiate at a wedding where one partner isn't Jewish. But even if I had known that at the time, it wouldn't have been the right decision for us.

How about a co-officiated wedding? I think the word "officiated" is very appropriate. With all the negotiating we were doing, I expected a guy in a black-and-white striped shirt and yellow flag to marry us. We thought it would be hard to find two clergy who would agree to jointly conduct a wedding service and who see their role in conducting an intermarriage wedding as proper. Although we felt that we could eventually find the right two people, we decided that this approach didn't make us comfortable. With the ceremony divided into a Jewish part and a Christian part, we just couldn't envision there being any flow to the service. It may work for some couples, but it was not our style. Then there was the issue of where to hold the wedding. For the same reasons, we didn't feel it would be fair to one of us if the ceremony were held in either a church or a synagogue.

We could see why everyone told us that interfaith marriages were difficult. Sometimes it crossed our minds that we had to be crazy to even attempt such a feat, but our love for each other kept us determined. Then one day, we found the perfect solution. A friend of Bonnie's mom, named Sheila, was a justice of the peace who performed civil ceremonies. She also happened to be a cantor, the person who leads the synagogue services in song. She specialized in officiating at weddings between interfaith couples and happily agreed to involve God in the wedding service. As a bonus, she was able to perform the songs in our wedding.

Sheila suggested that a nice hotel would be a warm and friendly neutral location to hold the service. This worked out well for the reception, too. We were able to incorporate some Jewish elements, such as the chuppah and the breaking of the glass. We even danced to a traditional Jewish tune called the *freilach*. I was worried that my Protestant friends and family would be lost, but to my surprise, this dance really energized the crowd and set a festive tone for the rest of the afternoon. Because these were mostly cultural and not religious details, my family did not feel threatened. As much as it was important that Bonnie and I planned the wedding based on our tastes, these are family affairs, and everyone should be made to feel as welcome as possible.

Having figured out the *how* and the *where*, we were faced with the question of *who* would show up. Many of my wife's relatives were Orthodox and did not approve of our marriage. Her great-uncle, for example, politely declined our invitation. At first, I was upset—no, angry. I thought it was insulting. However, after thinking about it for a few days, I came to understand his position. Her great-uncle was deeply rooted in his faith, which told him that intermarriage was not appropriate. Although we'd miss him, I now had a new respect for the man, who stood for what he thought was right.

More importantly, however, Bonnie's grandmother was riding the fence as to whether she would attend. To Bonnie, a wedding without her *bubba* would be like apples without honey on Rosh Hashanah, only on a much bigger scale. Ever since my wife had broken the news to her grandmother that we were getting married, Bubba had said that she wished her well but was not sure she would come to the wedding. I had been upset by her response, but as I cooled down, I was able to respect her beliefs. However, Bubba not coming to our wedding was different from Bonnie's great-uncle's decision. I did not really know him. I did know her grandmother, though. And I knew how much it would crush Bonnie if Bubba were not there. By this time, I was feeling anxious. This had become a big issue for me too.

Fortunately, thanks to some heart-to-heart talks with Bonnie's stepmother, Bubba decided that what was most important was her granddaughter's happiness. She came to the wedding. She even danced with me that wonderful summer afternoon. And while the Bo Winnaker Band played Benny Goodman's "Memories of You," I'll never forget what she said to me: "Jim, you're my grandson now."

OTHER VOICES

Julia and Mitchell, a newly engaged interfaith couple, set aside an evening to discuss their dreams for their wedding day. Before the discussion, they each made a list of all the things they considered most important—both during the ceremony and the reception. They then circled the top three most important items on their list. After that, Julia turned her paper over and listed all the things that she thought would be most important to Mitchell, and he did the same for her. At that point they discussed these lists, beginning with what each thought would be most important to their partner. The conversation enabled them to feel that they were sensitive to each other's needs. Julia and Mitchell talked about compromises each might be willing to make so they could have two of their top three needs met on their wedding day.

Since they actually had fun doing this exercise and felt that they had really communicated well, they each proceeded to make another list of the things they thought were most important to each partner's parents/family. They discussed possible ways to meet at least one of each of their family's top needs. They were amazed at how far they had come planning a near-perfect wedding.

Through this strategy, Mitchell gained an understanding of both the Swedish and Lutheran traditions that Julia valued; she understood the elements of a Jewish ceremony that were important to Mitchell. They had separated out what they wanted for their wedding versus what their parents wanted but had found ways to enable both sets of parents to feel comfortable and involved. Julia and Mitchell ended their discussion with an expression of appreciation to each other, feeling that they had strengthened their communication and learned about their partner's needs by listening with love and caring.

CHAPTER 7

How This Christian Came to Give His Daughters Hebrew Names

Once we had finally agreed on how we would raise our children, I began to grow comfortable with our decision.

"You know, they'll celebrate Hanukkah, not Christmas," my wife stated.

"Sure," I replied with confidence.

"They're going to go to temple, not church."

"I would expect that."

"If we have a girl, she'll have a *b'rit bat*."

"That's the baby-naming ceremony, right? It'll be beautiful."

"If we have a boy, he'll have a *b'rit milah*."

"No probl . . . Wait. Isn't that where they cut the . . . ?"

"Mmmhmm."

We ended up having two girls. However, back then, I spent a few moments pondering what I had gotten myself into. I had no problem with the idea of circumcision itself. I had been; why shouldn't my son be? It was just the idea of making a big deal out of the procedure that made me pause and wonder. In my imagination, I pictured all of our family and friends gathered in our living room, eating delicious food, engaging in lively conversation, and genuinely enjoying themselves. Then the mohel, who performs the ritual, steps up to the baby, pulls out his scissors, and SNIP! Bonnie's family shouts, "*Mazal tov!*" My family becomes silent—wide-eyed—frozen like deer in your headlights—then runs to the bathroom to recycle their sesame bagels.

I decided that a commitment was a commitment. My wife and I had made our decision together, and we would stick to it. If we had boys, we would just have to ease my family into the idea of the *b'rit milah*, or bris, as it is often called.

When joining two families of different faiths together, nothing else screams, "Welcome to intermarriage!" quite like a *b'rit milah*. Fortunately, my family has been very supportive every step of the way, and I'm sure they'd have behaved just fine if we had had a son. My guess was that they would have been so overjoyed just to have a grandson to love (and spoil) that nothing else would have mattered.

As it turns out, God has yet to test us on our reactions to a bris. Instead, God has given Bonnie and me two beautiful girls, for whom we had baby namings. While no surgery is involved during this ceremony, a *b'rit bat* is still a uniquely Jewish moment that can be foreign to a Protestant family such as mine. Interestingly, it can be new to many American Jews, as well, for the types of ceremonies in which Jewish baby girls are named today are elaborations on the way girls were generally named in past generations.

The first time I ever heard of a baby naming, I thought, "What's the deal with that? Didn't the parents already name her at the hospital? Why do they have to name her again?" As my wife explained, this is to give the daughter her Hebrew name. She also said that because today's baby namings are outgrowths of an older, simpler ritual, there is a lot of flexibility regarding what we could do for a ceremony. If we had had a boy and a *b'rit milah*, there would have been plenty of precedent to follow. Although the only part that is commanded in the Torah is the circumcision, a bris has many long-standing traditions. On the other hand, there are no steadfast rules for celebrating the birth of a daughter. The baby namings of previous generations were simple ceremonies at the synagogue and usually did not involve the female members of the family. Today's *b'rit bat* in America has evolved into a celebration that includes the whole family. It can be held in the home or in the synagogue. In our case, we chose to have the baby naming in our home, so my family would feel more comfortable.

Before our first daughter was born, we had decided what all her names were to be and after whom she would be named. We knew that we wanted to incorporate the names of our grandmothers, who had recently passed away. My wife told me that it is customary for Ashkenazic, or Eastern European, Jews to name their children after a deceased member of the family as a way of remembering them.

"Ah, that's why you don't see a lot of 'Juniors' in Jewish boys' names," I surmised. But wait a minute, we could have a problem.

"What about when you want to name your child after someone with a name that's, let's just say, no longer in style—like your grandmother, Gertrude?" I asked.

"Or your grandmother, Mildred?" she added.

"Yeah, I don't want her to get teased at school or called 'Mildew.'"

Bonnie explained that it is a common custom in the United States for families to use just the first letter of the ancestor's Hebrew name. She said, "Gertrude's 'Hebrew' name was Gittel (which is actually Yiddish). So for our daughter, we could take the 'G' from Gittel to make Gabrielle for the English name."

"Oh, so it's a loophole!" I replied.

For our second daughter, we used this "loophole" again and named her Molly, after my grandma Mildred. For the Hebrew name we chose Chava, which means "life" or lively" (turns out we were more than right with this one) and is the Hebrew equivalent of Eve. I'm sure if my grandma had been Jewish, this would have been *her* Hebrew name. This was also a nice opportunity to give Molly a Hebrew name belonging to another one of my wife's grandmothers. We felt it would be more appropriate to use this existing Hebrew name rather than make one up for the name Molly. Bottom line, I learned that there are a lot of acceptable ways to come up with names in the Jewish tradition.

The order of events for the baby namings of our two daughters went something like this: Friends and family arrived at our home and began to mingle while waiting for the rabbi to begin. At noon, the rabbi was ready to start. But some of *my* family and friends weren't there yet. They were, as usual, sociably late. We had forgotten to tell them that this is one occasion where it is not fashionable to be tardy.

Because it was a learning experience for many of the guests who attended our daughters' baby namings, I think that most were fascinated by it. The rabbi who came to our home to perform the ceremony did an excellent job of explaining what was about to take place. After welcoming all of our friends and family, he told everyone the significance of the baby naming. This was great for both Christians and Jews who had never witnessed one before. After my parents carried our daughter into the room, the rabbi gave her the Hebrew name we had selected. He then led us in a prayer that thanked God for sustaining us and bringing us to this moment. This prayer, known as the Shehecheyanu, is said at many Jewish get-togethers. The rabbi then had us all say the blessing for daughters: "May God make you as Sarah, Rebekah, Rachel, and Leah." Because these blessings were spoken in Hebrew, he fortunately made them repeat-after-me prayers. He then gave us the English translations. The rabbi concluded with a blessing that recognized that our daughter was entering the covenant with God and that our hopes were for her to love learning through study of the Torah, be happy, be respectful, and act in honest and ethical ways.

One of my worst fears, when we informed my parents that we would raise our children Jewish, was that they would say, "That's fine; just not too Jewish." Having a rabbi hold your daughter and pray that she would study Torah can be a little overwhelming for a Christian dad hearing it for the first time, as well as for a Christian grandparent. This was definitely our first test. Happily, my parents were eagerly engaged in the ceremony, joyful just to be part of their granddaughter's life.

When the rabbi finished, my in-laws said the blessings over the wine and challah. The participation of both sets of grandparents was not only beautiful, but also crucial. Bonnie and I had coordinated what would take place ahead of time. We wanted to make sure that both families felt at home and comfortable with the ceremony. By having Bonnie's parents say the blessings and my parents carry our daughter into the room, everyone was a part of the baby naming.

Nothing but smiles adorned the faces of those who were in our living room on both of those occasions. Instead of potentially alienating my family, the baby namings resoundingly opened the door and welcomed them into our daughters' Jewish life. Looking back, I think that my wife and I were the only ones who were nervous. During our first daughter's ceremony, I remember not wanting to mess up. I could just hear my Jewish in-laws: "There he goes messing up one of our fine traditions." (For the record, though, I don't really believe anyone would have thought that.)

After the rabbi gave our daughters their names, my wife and I each wanted to say a few words about why we chose these names, the people after whom they were named, and what their Hebrew names meant to us. In both ceremonies though, Bonnie was too emotional to speak, so it was up to me to do the talking. I began by telling everyone how we felt about the meanings of these names and how we hoped our daughters could emulate their loving great-grandmothers. I felt much more confident for my second daughter's naming three years later. You should have heard me pronounce "Chava."

After the ceremony, it was, of course, time to enjoy the delicious spread of food covering the dining room table. Bagels, lox, pastries, cheeses, noodle kugel—you name it, we ate it. Like most Jewish get-togethers, it just wouldn't be official without the food. Everyone was laughing, talking, and eating. I didn't care that it was thirty degrees and snowing outside. As far as I was concerned, it was a gorgeous day.

I'm sure that if we had had boys, each *b'rit milah* would have been just as fulfilling. Right now, though, I'm just as happy letting my friends with boys have the honors.

I'll never forget either of our daughters' baby namings, but the first one struck me as incredibly significant. The days leading up to the *b'rit bat* were a little nerve-racking for me. This was really it—the commencement of raising our daughter in Judaism. I was about to give her a type of name that I did not have. Was I going to feel connected to my wife and child? Then, I realized: this was *my* daughter. She was a part of *me*. On the day of the baby naming, it all came together for me. There I was, standing in my living room, a Christian, in the middle of a Jewish ceremony expounding on these Hebrew names. I looked out at the room full of loved ones. I looked down at my daughter's sweet face. I couldn't have felt more at home.

CHAPTER 8

Bat Mitzvah: The Natural Next Step

When our synagogue gave us the date for Gabbi's bat mitzvah, it was a big moment for all of us—our baby was growing up. After recovering from this exciting news (and the shock it sent me into), we began making arrangements for her big day. While it seemed completely natural that she would become a bat mitzvah, I had to pause and marvel at how far our interfaith family had come.

There was never any question as to whether we'd be able to figure out how to go through the bat mitzvah process. We knew we could do it. We had been members of Temple Beth Emeth for years and were completely immersed in the religious education of our daughters. I, the dad, the non-Jew, had become extremely comfortable with raising Jewish children. If someone had told me back when Bonnie and I were trying to figure out our religious and cultural differences that I would one day be enthusiastically engaged in helping my daughter through this major life-cycle event, I would have said, "How much did my Jewish in-laws pay you to say that?"

It helped that we belonged to a diverse and welcoming synagogue. I noticed that our family was by no means the first interfaith family to have a bat mitzvah in the temple, so I didn't feel like an outcast. We also had many intermarried friends going through the process, which put us in good company.

We were lucky, however. Friends of ours who belonged to another temple in town were in fact facing problems. At their synagogue, the non-Jewish father would not be allowed on the *bimah* while the Torah was open and people were reading from it. Personally, I couldn't fathom not being up there with my daughter on such a momentous life event. I had raised her, driven her back and forth to religious school, helped her study, joined in Jewish religious celebrations and services, and volunteered at our temple. And then to be told that I couldn't stand next to her on the *bimah*? My friend and his wife felt the same way and decided to join our temple instead, where the non-Jewish spouse is included on the *bimah*.

Fortunately, I didn't have to go through such a gut-wrenching decision as they did. My road to Gabbi's bat mitzvah seemed a lot smoother. However, it did remind me that many interfaith families still face a lot of hurdles.

Once we had Gabbi's date, our family jumped right in and began planning. I made sure to learn as much as I could about what our temple requires Gabbi to do and what our roles were to be during the service. I never had a bar mitzvah or anything close to it. This is a uniquely Jewish thing. I was amazed by everything that she was supposed to do: to know Hebrew well enough to chant her portions from the Torah and *Haftarah*; to be able to sing the blessings before and after her Torah and *Haftarah* portions; to give a speech about the meaning of and her reflections on the Torah portion; and to complete a charity/volunteer (mitzvah) project.

My job assisting Bonnie with things like invitations and

venue was relatively easy. The bigger question was whether Gabbi was ready for her part in the service. Was she ready to become an adult in Judaism's eyes?

During the final month before her bat mitzvah, we had yet to nail down the final number of attendees, the last couple of menu items, and what tie I would wear. And Gabbi hadn't finished her own preparations either, although she was close. She had learned her Torah portion, her *Haftarah*, and the blessings. She was chanting very well when she practiced. However, she needed to finish writing her speech. She'd been typing away on the computer and conferring with Rabbi Levy; however, her speech still required a bit more body, editing, and refining. I knew she understood the meaning of her Torah portion—it was just a matter of putting it all into her own words. Gabbi had already done a lot of work on her bat mitzvah overall. She was taking it seriously and didn't complain . . . much.

Since I never had a bar mitzvah, I wondered how our daughter (or anybody this age) would be ready to chant in a foreign language to a room full of people, including her seventh-grade classmates. I remembered how my singing sounded during puberty. I would have been terrified! Fortunately, Gabbi had a beautiful voice. I also remembered that my maturity level at that age would've made it hard for me to fulfill all of our temple's requirements.

More importantly, was Gabbi ready to take on the responsibilities that Judaism was asking of her? Was she going to contribute meaningfully to temple life? To society? Was she ready to perform *mitzvot*? As Bonnie and I tried to figure out how to parent our way through the adolescent years, we chuckled a bit and said, "Hmmm." That is, sometimes we would think that Gabbi's maturity was a ways away, and sometimes we would see

Gabbi perform with the grace and poise of Princess Diana.

Bonnie often said that she saw a big neon sign above Gabbi's head that read: "Work in Progress." I don't know what my wife had been eating to cause her to have these hallucinations, but I thought I understood the general idea. Right before Passover, Gabbi spent all her allowance money on chocolate, pretzels, and lip-gloss at the mall. Then, just a few days later, came this sudden flash of maturity and compassion. During the second seder, her grandmother (who had just lost her mother) was telling us about charitable donations she wanted to make in her mother's memory that would provide therapy dogs to nursing homes. Gabbi piped up, "I'll be happy to donate some of my bat mitzvah money to that." These words were a comforting ray of sunshine to her grandmother (and to us).

As I looked at our daughter with admiration (if not a bit of shock), this neon glow started to materialize above her head. Suddenly I saw these words: "Making Progress." I was hoping that in a few weeks on the *bimah*, another sign would glow: "Introducing Gabbi 2.0."

In addition to studying for the service, Gabbi was expected to take on a mitzvah project—that is, a project that helps someone in some way. Our daughter, who has a passion for reading, chose to help set up a program to provide books for low-income parents to read to their children.

I had heard that bar and bat mitzvah students typically had their work cut out for them. Was that ever an understatement! Gabbi's workload reminded me of the time in college when I already had a full schedule and then took on another three-credit course. Her mitzvah project took a lot of planning and hard work. The boy Gabbi partnered with for her big day was a very capable young man. Together, the two of them helped the boy's mother, a pediatrician, establish a Reach Out and Read program at her office. The tenets of the program enabled pediatricians to provide children's books to low-income families and then encourage the parents to read to their children.

Why was this important? Through research, Gabbi found that people who are literate are healthier. They are able to read instructions on medicine boxes, and they are more likely to be informed about public health hazards. The best way to jump-start literacy is for parents to start reading to their children at an early age.

I think that Gabbi said it best in her speech: "If you give a man a book, you don't really do much for him. If you teach a man to read, you open up lots of opportunities for him. This is not quite as catchy as the original saying about fish, but it is true all the same." As for the Reach Out and Read program, Gabbi said, "Here we are not only providing the fish, but the rod and the bait as well."

As a parent, you always hope that your children grow to be compassionate and selfless. I was very proud of what she had accomplished. To be honest, when I was their age, helping the community like this was not anywhere on my radar. My brain was trying to figure out school, relationships, being just cool enough, and what my changing body was doing. I never thought I would have enough room or time to spend helping others. Gabbi showed me that young people could find the time and have the excitement to perform good deeds. She, through this Jewish rite of passage, was also showing me something that I never knew when I was her age—adolescents can be very capable of doing their part in the synagogue and the greater community.

While Gabbi was taking care of her end of the bat mitzvah, I was doing my best to be helpful and supportive to everyone.

This included helping to plan the party after the service. If I had had to plan it by myself, Kentucky Fried Chicken would probably cater the party, and the entertainment would be the NHL playoffs on TV. Bonnie knew this and had graciously taken charge. Fortunately for Gabbi, her mom had had her own bat mitzvah and had a better grip on what needed to be done.

One of the first things that my wife told me that many people do is pick a theme and tone for the party. (Theme? Wasn't the theme Judaism?) I have discovered that there is a ton of pressure to entertain these middle school kids. They want a party worthy of the Oscars. Nonetheless, in sticking with a style that wouldn't scare off our relatives, Gabbi, Bonnie, and I decided to have a fun party, but not "over the top." We did hire a DJ and an energetic party leader who had dance moves and could get the crowd fired up. It was either that or go with some guy and his pet parakeet we saw on www.MyParentsAreLame.com.

While hiring a total stranger to get our guests onto the dance floor seemed very odd to me, imagine trying to explain this system to my Protestant side of the family. I had been telling them that the workload in planning a bat mitzvah was somewhere between a birthday party and a wedding. They usually just politely nodded their heads. I then would tell them that we also had to reserve a venue, hire a photographer, and find a florist. The more I thought about it, this was getting a lot closer to a wedding.

Even though I had no experience in planning a bat mitzvah, I wanted to be an equal partner in helping out, whether I was Jewish or not. I had been very active in bringing up our daughters—in both their secular and religious lives—so this desire came naturally to me.

Although getting ready for Gabbi's big day was a learning

curve for me, I felt that we now had a good handle on the situation. We had a great checklist of what had to be done and by when. We knew what the theme would be, and we had reserved the venue. (Now, if we could just get our daughter to finish her speech.)

I understood that becoming a bat mitzvah was a big rite of passage for Gabbi. This may have been a lot for a Protestant dad to grasp, but the only thing that I really needed to know was that when I saw my daughter on the *bimah*, I would be the proudest dad on earth. That would require no planning at all.

Finally, the big day had arrived. My daughter's bat mitzvah was a fantastic experience for our whole interfaith family. To hear Gabbi on the *bimah* chanting her Torah portion, to see her mature into this young woman, and to see my Protestant family joyfully embrace its first bat mitzvah—all I could say was, "Wow! It couldn't have been better."

I guess, not being Jewish, I didn't have too many expectations for Gabbi's big day. However, I had been to a few bar and bat mitzvah celebrations on my wife's side of the family, which enabled me to know what typical services and subsequent celebrations were like. Still, when it's your own daughter, unexpected feelings seem to surface. The first emotion I felt while she was preparing was amazement—awe at how much she had to learn, wonder at how I would have handled the workload if I were in her shoes. Then I felt a bit of anxiety. Could she pull it off? Why didn't she just finish her speech already? When she finally pulled it all together in the final two weeks, my mood shifted to relief and confidence that she would do just fine.

Is surreal an emotion? If it is, then that's how I would describe my feelings during the rehearsal (yes, rehearsal; see, Mom, it is like a wedding). The moment came when Rabbi Levy was showing Gabbi how to fold her tallit. I started thinking to myself, "This is really happening. Our little girl is becoming a bat mitzvah!" Upon initial reflection, that felt a little weird, as I'm not even Jewish. Why should I get so *verklempt*? However, it did mean as much to me as to her Jewish mother. I'm her father. I've been a fifty-fifty partner with her mother in raising Gabbi—in the secular world as well as the religious. You might say that I had a lot invested here, but it's not about me. I think love describes it more accurately. I always want her to succeed and grow as a person.

It would be an understatement to say that the bat mitzvah was a meaningful event. Despite this being my side's first ever, there was no holding back. We asked my parents to take part in the service, and they eagerly accepted. Their job was to "dress" the Torah—which means putting the cover and ornamental pieces back on it after the Torah service. Of course, they were a little nervous about what to do, but they had known Rabbi Levy for years, and he was very understanding and accommodating. He has helped many interfaith families through this process and was able to help them along. It really touched me that my parents were so willing to take part. When looking back, however, I realize that their participation came as naturally to them as mine had. I attribute this to those early days in my relationship with Bonnie, when we made it clear that we wanted the grandparents to be a part of their grandkids' lives. Ever since then, my parents have been comfortable with any and all aspects of our daughters' religious lives. The bat mitzvah was the natural next step for them, too.

At the evening party, the spirit continued. The kids had fun, the adults had fun, and both sides jumped right in on dancing the hora. When the party ended, everyone was still smiling.

It's funny—I tried for weeks to give my parents and siblings a heads-up on what to expect at a bat mitzvah, but their eyes still teared up during the service. They were proud of Gabbi for her accomplishment. The fact that it was a Jewish ceremony did not matter to them. It was a big deal to Gabbi and therefore a big deal to them. When you stop thinking about the differences, love is all that matters.

The joy that we all felt from that blissful bat mitzvah afterglow would have to last us until sister Molly's three years later. It was then that we were blessed to be able to experience the whole process over again. And even though I had more of an idea of what to expect that time, my emotions for Molly's rite of passage were just as strong.

CHAPTER 9

Losing a Loved One

Thankfully, neither Bonnie nor I have yet lost a loved one in our immediate family. Just because death has not entered our household yet, however, doesn't mean that we haven't talked about it. It's not like we're obsessed with the subject, but we do feel it necessary to have a plan. You never know when exactly you're going to have to "make arrangements." When the day comes, what will we do?

The Jewish and Christian faiths have different rituals for dealing with death. For interfaith families, there is no well-established precedent. After she's gone, it's awfully hard to ask your spouse, "Do you want the rabbi to perform your eulogy?" Or, "How do you want us to mourn for you?" Or to find out, "I always expected that we'd be laid to rest where my grandparents are. I didn't know it was a Christian cemetery."

There are so many details to figure out that it does no good to wait until it's too late. It's like having a will—it's depressing to have to think about it, but it's got to be done. Talk about it, even put your thoughts to paper, get it over with, and then you don't have to worry about it—the matter is settled.

In stark contrast, if you take a look at weddings, details are often imagined even before people are engaged. Many young people have dreamed about how every aspect of their wedding would turn out. They always wanted an outdoor wedding, or they really had their hearts set on being married at sea on a cruise. They'd serve white chocolate desserts shaped like swans, smothered with raspberry sauce, or have a big barbeque on the lawn. But when it comes to death, funerals, and mourning, many people don't take the time to plan ahead. Why? Let's face—it's not exactly a fun subject to dream about.

For couples who share the same faith, planning ahead is important, but many of the rituals are well-established, according to their religion. Although it doesn't prevent disagreements on what to do when a loved one dies, people have a general picture of what to expect. They'll be buried in a Jewish cemetery. The immediate family will sit shiva (the Jewish period of mourning). For some Christians, there will be an open-casket viewing (something not done by Jews). Or there will be a traditional Irish wake or whatever is the family's custom.

The interfaith couple, on the other hand, cannot afford to leave the details to chance. Just like the other life-cycle events that they had so meticulously planned out, making sure that both religions were considered, that both sets of in-laws were accommodated, that the moment reflected their dual-faith lifestyle in a consistent manner, the interfaith couple must be ready for the last of the life-cycle events—death.

Bonnie and I felt that as painful as it was to think about, we needed to consider what we would do. Where would be the best place for burial that would accept Christians and Jews? Is cremation an option? Would I, the Christian, want to sit shiva for her? If something happened to us while our children were young, who would take them in? Would they continue to be raised Jewish? As we get older, our specifics have changed, but we know that we have to start discussing the framework now. The first thing we needed to do was to understand what our religious traditions expected of us.

I've noticed that Protestant funerals are often of the same structure as our weddings—loose. There are a few traditions to follow, but generally speaking, the procedures are basic. Most of the time, there is a reception or viewing at the funeral home. Usually a day later, there is a funeral service at the funeral home or church. There is no standard time frame in which to hold these.

During the Protestant service, someone, usually a minister, friend, or family member, performs the eulogy, or remembrance. This is a speech to celebrate the life of the deceased, to speak of him or her in an upbeat way, and to provide comfort for the grieving. Sometimes more than one person gives a remembrance. Prayers are recited, including the Lord's Prayer. Often a hymn or two are sung.

After the funeral service, a procession leads to the cemetery or other resting place, for the final committal. Most often, the minister says a few more words, including the recitation of a traditional psalm. Another prayer is said. Then the grieving friends and family retreat to the funeral parlor or home of the deceased for a reception. At the cemetery, sometimes the casket is lowered into the ground after the family leaves. Sometimes it is lowered while everyone is still gathered.

The Jewish practice is somewhat similar, but with different prayers and a few extra traditions. One big difference is that Jewish law requires that the body be buried within twenty-four hours or as soon as possible after that. (Protestants often will wait longer to bury.) Just before the funeral service, the immediate family "cuts *k'ri'ah*." This is the symbolic tearing of clothes representing the tear in their lives caused by the death of the loved one. Generally, the funeral home will provide a black ribbon to cut as a substitute. Many Jews also wish to be buried covered in a shroud. Jewish families traditionally choose a plain pine box or at least a wooden casket instead of something more elaborate.

There is no set liturgy for a Jewish service, though a selection of psalms are recited. The rabbi is often the one who gives the eulogy, or *hespeid*, as it is called in Hebrew, although sometimes family members or friends do it. A Jewish service will also often include poems or meditative readings. The service ends with the chanting of El Malei Rachamim—a prayer asking God to give rest to the soul. Then everyone proceeds to the burial site. After additional readings, and once the casket has been lowered, the Mourner's Kaddish is recited.

Jewish and Protestant funeral procedures are both basic. They have a minimum number of rules to observe. Where the big difference lies between the two is in the numerous customs that surround Jewish death and mourning. Many of the Jewish traditions originate from traditional practices and are modified or reinterpreted by Conservative or Reform Jews. Take, for instance, cutting *k'ri'ah*. Some Orthodox Jews will cut their actual clothes. Most Reform Jews cut a black ribbon and pin it to their clothes. Either way, the ritual is considered fulfilled.

When Bonnie's grandmother in Rhode Island passed away, we observed and participated in many of these traditional rituals. After her casket was lowered into the ground, we each took a turn with the shovel, throwing dirt into the grave in a symbolic act of closure, seen by Jewish tradition as a final act of caring for the dead.

When we returned from the cemetery, we all washed our

hands—not because they were dirty from shoveling, but because we were taking part in another tradition. This one grows out of superstition and has different meanings to different people. For us, it was to wash our hands of any impurity connected to the cemetery or death itself.

Back at her grandmother's house, I noticed that all of the mirrors were covered. Bonnie explained to me that this was so that people wouldn't be tempted to peer into them to see how they looked. It is a traditional custom for those in mourning to not shave or put on makeup, another aspect of not thinking about one's appearance. There are also ancient superstitions associated with covering the mirrors. Today many Jews leave their mirrors uncovered, because they view the tradition as unnecessary or archaic.

For seven days, Bonnie's father sat shiva in his mother's house. I found it incredibly therapeutic to be able to mourn with family and friends for more than just one day. Sure, most people grieve for a long time, but to actually have a tradition to follow for a set period of days was comforting. We received extended family and well-wishers throughout the week. They brought lots of food and conversation. It was also beautiful to witness how many people cared for Bubba.

Bonnie took part in each of these traditions. This is how she was raised. This is what she is used to. These practices have helped her and her parents grieve in years past.

She and I have talked about how sitting shiva would be a helpful process for our family. If I pass away first, she and our daughters would sit shiva for me, even though I am Christian and will probably have a ceremony that recognizes that in some way. In mourning, I'd expect my wife and daughters to follow any of the Jewish customs and laws that they wanted. They will be the ones grieving, not me. If she passes away first, I expect that I would sit shiva with Gabbi and Molly for their mother. We have made a commitment to have a Jewish home. These are Jewish traditions that are designed to help the grieving. My side of the family would be more than welcome to participate but would also be allowed to grieve in any manner in which they feel comfortable.

I imagine that my family would see the beauty in these Jewish rituals, laws, and customs of mourning, just as I have come to appreciate them. They are designed to comfort the grieving friends and family. I also expect that when my Christian parents pass away, my wife, daughters, and I will grieve together in a very Jewish way. Sometimes, during a period of great stress, it's hard to play things by ear. It's nice to know what you are expected to do.

I find that the timeline provided by the stages of the Jewish mourning process are psychologically uplifting. Shiva is for seven days—no more. After that, you are expected to start coming out of the house and getting on with life. Another part of Jewish mourning is the thirty-day period of *sh'loshim*. This includes the first seven days (shiva) and twenty-three more. During those twenty-three days, the grieving family slowly reacclimatizes itself back into the world outside of the house. The family is still expected to recite Kaddish daily but is allowed to return to work. Getting out and meeting with people is encouraged, as long as it is not a party, entertainment function, or sporting event.

Before the end of the first year, the family may have an "unveiling." This is a Jewish custom of holding a religious ceremony at the cemetery to unveil the deceased's gravestone. Remembering the one-year mark of the person's death is referred to as *yahrtzeit*. It is observed annually by saying Kaddish and lighting a *yahrtzeit* candle, which burns for twenty-four hours.

These Jewish customs help the family in times of emotional stress, without letting them wallow in a morbid atmosphere. They slowly encourage the mourners to reenter the world of the living, while still honoring the memory of their departed loved one.

How it all actually works out for us remains to be seen. But at least Bonnie and I have started the ball rolling. Talking to our clergy has also been helpful. If nothing else, making the appointments to see the rabbi and minister provided initiative and an abundance of information as to what our options are—especially regarding the services and cemetery restrictions. We were relieved to find out that the rabbi and minister were open to working with our unique needs. Both have dealt with interfaith families like ours. They have given us numerous ideas about what to do when the day comes. But most of all, they have let us know that they care and will help us.

Part III

PARENTING

CHAPTER 10

Questions about God from the Backseat

"Daddy, you know everything, don't you?" is something you would think a guy likes to hear from his kids. At first, my head swelled to fill the interior of the minivan I was driving on the way to preschool. Gabbi, then five years old, had just floated this softball of a statement as a distraction to catch me off guard for what she really wanted to ask.

As I tried to explain to her that while I do know a lot, I do not know everything, she couldn't wait to interrupt me with her first question.

"Daddy, when does water become ice?"

"When the temperature gets to thirty-two degrees or colder, the water freezes to form ice."

"Daddy, why are leaves green?"

"Well, that's because they're full of chlorophyll, which is used by the tree to convert sunlight into food." ("This is easy. Maybe I do know everything," I thought.)

Then came the sneak attack. "Daddy, what is God?"

As I fumbled my way through the best impromptu answer I could think of, I couldn't help but wish that my wife were there to help me field this one. My daughter had suddenly become the press corps, and I was the White House press secretary.

I knew that whatever I told her needed to be good because she would take this information and use it as a building block to form her images of God and her Jewish religion. I was worried that if I gave the wrong answer, I could give her a warped sense of what or who God is. Or worse, I could turn her away from religion and a belief in God forever. Where was my parenting manual when I needed it?

To top it all off, I, as the Christian parent of the family, had to give my daughter an explanation that would be satisfactory according to Judaism. In addition, it would have to meet her mother's own image of God. My wife and I had never really discussed the topic of how we would explain God to our kids. Our many discussions about how to raise children in an interfaith family had not prepared me for this very moment.

I had probably envisioned Gabbi, at a much older age, scheduling an appointment to see my wife and me to discuss the meaning of God. "Mom, Dad? I want to have a chat about God with you. How's next Tuesday at 9:30 sound?" This would have given us plenty of time to prepare our answer. Then we could have presented a united front with a consistent message. Unfortunately, at that moment in the minivan, in the middle of traffic on Eisenhower Parkway, I had to hope that what I told Gabbi, without any preparation, was not only correct, but also what her mother would have wanted her to hear.

At least I had made the decision to tell my daughter something that would be consistent with her faith and not mine. I had decided that it would not be appropriate to try and discuss my belief in Jesus and how He relates to God. If there's one thing that my wife and I had previously agreed upon, it was to make sure that our daughters receive a Jewish education and know that they are not both Jewish and Christian. I remember thinking that one day they're going to be curious and ask me about my religion, and I'll tell them. After all, the more they know about other religions, the more educated and tolerant they'll be.

Fortunately, my wife and I have always believed the Judeo-Christian God to be the same God. From this viewpoint, I found it easier to simply relate my view of God, as my parents and ministers had taught me, and how I had molded my belief in God over the years. I had to laugh as I briefly thought of what an ancient Roman and Jewish interfaith family would have gone through. At least neither one of us was polytheistic. So, instead of focusing on the differences between Judaism and Christianity, I kept my discussion to the commonalities of our belief in God. "There is only one God. God is everywhere. God is a loving God." To which she replied, "Oh. Can we have ice cream tonight?"

In the end, I found the interfaith issue to not be as difficult as I thought it would be. What turned out to be the most challenging was taking a step back and examining my own view of God. While I have always believed in God, I haven't ever tried to explain the concept to anyone—especially a five-year-old, whom it was my duty to teach. Somehow I managed to find a way, and each day I get a little better at it.

I knew that my daughter's religious education would not end with that one discussion we had in the car. It would continue throughout her life. In fact, since then, Gabbi, her sister Molly, and I have had a few more talks about God. I have also taught them about my belief in Jesus. Surprisingly, they seem to be unfazed by it. Hopefully, that's due to a consistent Jewish message from her mother and me. They understand that they are Jewish and their tradition believes one thing, whereas my Christian tradition believes something else. I find the experience of being part of their education refreshing and rewarding, not just in teaching them, but also in reaffirming my own belief in God.

OTHER VOICES

Talking about God is challenging for most parents and often even more challenging for parents from two different faith backgrounds. It helps to have discussions early on as a couple about the importance of religion in your life, long before your children are old enough to ask their own questions. Consider the classic story of the little boy who goes down the street to play with the slightly older new kid who has just moved in. Upon returning home, he asks his parents, "Where do I come from?" While they thought they had a year or two before they might have to deal with this question, it is obvious to them that the older boy has hastened the need for the talk. After the boy's parents go through a long explanation about the birds and the bees, the boy looks quizzically at his parents and says, "No, Johnny down the street comes from Cleveland. Where do I come from?"

There are no right or wrong answers, and what your children believe at age five will probably be very different from what they believe at age ten and different still from age fifteen. Rather than sharing factual information, God-talk opens up the opportunity for children to develop their own understanding of God. Though they may want to know what their parents think, one way to advance the conversation is to ask them what they believe. Children will often ask a question about a topic because they have an idea they want to share. When they ask about God, ask in return, "Tell me, what do you think about God?" This open-ended conversation may well open up a fruitful dialogue.

Speak honestly about your own beliefs, no matter how well developed or unresolved they may be. Expressing respect for the beliefs of your partner and your child is more important than having all the answers. It is fine, and can even be helpful, to show that you yourself have doubts or internal struggles about belief, but that you keep on asking the questions.

CHAPTER 11

"Don't They Know I'm Jewish?" Our Children Start to Comprehend Their Jewish Identity

I knew it was bound to happen. There was really no way to prevent it—not that I wanted to prevent it. What I'm referring to is the fact that our daughters' Jewish identities had started to come alive within them.

This thirst for knowledge has begun with Gabbi, who, being older and attending religious school on Saturdays, asked questions and made comments about her Jewish world that her mother and I hadn't expected. More than once her queries had caused Bonnie and me to look at each other and ask, "You wanna handle this one?" Most of the time, though, we were able to sufficiently answer our girls with responses that made sense to them and were consistent with our interfaith philosophy. Later, when we were alone, Bonnie and I would laugh hysterically at being caught off guard or at the humorous way in which the girls opined on a subject.

Even though kids do say the darndest things, not all of their comments are funny. The pure innocence of their remarks can be refreshing. Sometimes I feel their sorrow as they discover something about their Jewish identity that makes them feel sad.

One December when she was six, Gabbi had begun to notice that most people in our neighborhood didn't put menorahs in their windows. In fact, most of the trees in the yards of our street had Christmas lights. "Why are there so many Christmas lights? Where are the Hanukkah decorations?" she asked.

Gabbi's friend Claire, who is also growing up in an interfaith family, used to use the "light test" to determine who in her neighborhood was Jewish and who was Christian. "The houses with lights are the Christians, and the houses without lights are the Jews."

Claire's mom laughed as she told me how she tried to explain to Claire that that isn't always the case. "Unfortunately, it had given my daughter an inflated census count of the number of Jewish households."

One night while driving the girls home, I also tried to explain to Gabbi that in our country, there are quite a few more Christians than Jews. I could sense her shock and disbelief at my words. Sure, she had many Christian friends. She had met many more at her public school. She also knew full well that my side of the family is Christian. However, Gabbi had grown up going to the Jewish Community Center's preschool, and she also went to religious school at the temple. She just naturally assumed that because so many of the people she was around were Jewish, most of the rest of the world would be Jewish too.

Our younger daughter Molly, sitting in the seat next to her sister and in the midst of the "why stage," repeatedly asked why there were more Christians than Jews. I didn't have a clear-cut answer as to why. But I did let my daughters know that they certainly were not alone. I explained to them that being Jewish was something to be proud of. Like most things in life, it doesn't matter how many other people are like you. What's important is how good you are at being who you are and how you feel about being what you are.

Following that conversation, Gabbi and Molly began to realize that they were in a minority. However, there were times when I could see Gabbi getting a little miffed at the lack of attention given to her religion in American culture. Later that December, our family found ourselves in Boston's Quincy Market. As we walked with our cousins in and out of the stores and around the food stands, the atmosphere was festive. People laughed and scurried about, big shopping bags in hand. Pretty lights were strung up all over, wreaths hung on doors—some of the shops even had that fake frost painted in their window corners. It was the holiday season. It was the *Christmas* holiday season.

Suddenly, Gabbi exclaimed in disgust, "Ughhh! Don't they know I'm Jewish?"

As we stifled a laugh, Bonnie replied, "No, honey, they don't." But then, more sympathetically, "I know. Sometimes it stinks when there are no Jewish decorations."

Later that night, after the kids were in bed, Bonnie and I discussed how hard it could be to comfort our daughters on this subject and, at the same time, teach them the realities of being in a minority group. It's not always easy, or fun, to be different.

Given the dominant Christian culture in our society, I can see that it would be easy for our girls to want to be a part of it. This is particularly true when many of their friends are not Jewish. When Gabbi went to play at one of her Christian friend's houses, the talk between the two sometimes fell into a comparative exchange.

"I'm getting an American Girl doll for Christmas."

"Well, I'm getting one for Hanukkah."

"I get lots of presents on Christmas morning."

"Well I get presents for eight days."

Some things never change. I can remember having the same conversation with one of my Jewish friends in first grade.

Gabbi's Jewish friend Sarah had a Christian friend also named Sarah. The two Sarahs were inseparable. From what Gabbi's friend's mother told me, the two Sarahs' conversations during playdates got to be quite deep.

"How can you not believe in Jesus?"

"Are you going to heaven?"

They were naturally curious and open, trying to figure it all out. In the future, I expected to see a talk show titled "Religion Rap—with Your Hosts Sarah and Sarah." They needed to get through first grade though.

No matter how hard we tried to surround Gabbi and Molly with Jewish elements and protect them from being swallowed up by the dominant culture, we just couldn't isolate them. Going to a public school, they always had plenty of Christian friends and had been exposed to a variety of religions other than their own. Fortunately, the Ann Arbor public school system is sensitive to its diverse population. The teachers planned lessons that helped the kids learn about many different cultures. In addition, there were no Christmas pageants in which all the kids were required to participate.

I always laugh at the story that my father-in-law tells of when he was in kindergarten, singing in the Christmas concert of his Providence, Rhode Island, elementary school. "You should have seen the look on my mother's face," he relates, "especially when the teacher announced to the audience that I was to sing a solo of 'Silent Night.' Her jaw hit the floor. The next year, I was in Hebrew school."

One alternative for us would have been to send our daughters to the Jewish day school here in town. It is a fine school with a great reputation. There, our girls would have gotten a solid Jewish education and would have been surrounded by other Jewish children. However, Bonnie and I felt that in our case, Gabbi and Molly were getting a strong foundation in Judaism through the programs at the Jewish Community Center and at the synagogue. Besides, the public schools in our community have fantastic teachers and curricula. Growing up in Ann Arbor myself, I always felt that I gained tremendously by being in a setting where I could make friends with kids from different backgrounds.

There's no way for us to shelter our children from the dominant Christian culture—especially since I am Christian. They get plenty of Christianity from my side of the family as it is. And they seem to be doing just fine. I think what makes the difference is that Bonnie and I have worked extra hard to instill in them a Jewish identity. Perhaps, as an interfaith family, we have an advantage because we know we have to make a conscious effort. Yes, they learn a lot about my religion, but at the same time, we go to great lengths to teach them about Judaism. They know that even though their mother and I are of two different religions, they are not of both religions, and they seem comfortable with who they are. Rather than hiding from the reality of Christianity, we tackle it head-on by answering their questions. This way, they have the self-confidence to handle themselves and feel good about being Jewish, while not panicking just because a Christmas carol comes on the radio.

Nowhere is this more of a test than when my wife and daughters accompany me to church. Although their visits with me there are infrequent, Bonnie has confided to me that she worries about all the talk of Jesus during the service. When they were young, we wondered if it would confuse Gabbi and Molly. We just continued to instill in them that I am the Christian and, though they were there to keep me company, it was not their service or their house of worship.

By attending the many JCC and synagogue functions as a family, we drove the message home that they are Jewish girls in a Jewish family. It is through these activities that I find so much joy in seeing their Jewish identity soar. The year that Gabbi started her formal religious education at the temple—her first leg on the journey to becoming a bat mitzvah and taking on the responsibilities of a Jewish adult—I was very excited.

To be honest, when Bonnie and I discussed the religion of our future children before we were married, I wasn't sure that I could raise Jewish children—especially if it meant going through this coming-of-age ceremony. Was it the fear of the unknown? Was it concern over what my role, as the Christian father, would be in the process? I had been to only one bat mitzvah. I can remember thinking, "How on earth will I know how to help my kids through this?" Was it fear of what my Christian family would think? They might say, "Hey, Jim, we put up with you raising your children Jewish, but now you need to tone it down."

Looking back on it today, I have no idea why I was so afraid. And after Gabbi began her religious education, I couldn't imagine why she *wouldn't* become a bat mitzvah. Given how much she enjoyed going to religious school on Saturdays, she would probably have been eternally upset with me if I told her that she couldn't mark this milestone. It also would have been contrary to the plan that Bonnie and I had put forth to raise our children as Jews. If you're going to do something, you might as well do it right. I couldn't imagine feeling anything but the deep sense of pride I felt the day she became a woman in the eyes of the Jewish community.

I remember feeling that before she grew up too fast, I wanted to savor every moment of her burgeoning wonder at the world around her. I knew that she was going to ask more and more questions. I could only imagine our future conversations about religion. "Daddy, tell me more about Christianity." Or, "Daddy, do we believe in the same God?" She surprised me once with her questions. The next time, I planned to be ready and eager to answer her. I would tell her all that I knew and all that she would like to hear. Although we are of different religions, we share the same God. The gap between our two faiths narrowed a lot when I looked at it from that perspective. I hoped that she would find comfort in that thought, as well.

OTHER VOICES

A little girl with parents of different faiths burst into tears one afternoon, saying, "But Mommy, I am good." It was November, and a Christian cousin had explained that she was trying hard to be good so that Santa Claus would come. Through the child's eyes, issues like being good for Santa Claus can be very confusing, even when parents have made a clear choice of religious identity for the child. Many families do not have direct conversations on the subject of what it means to be an interfaith family. Children may learn songs, hear stories, and make crafts and food related to Jewish holidays at home and at the synagogue. At the same time, they may be exposed to other symbols, hear different songs, and experience other celebrations in the homes of grandparents and extended family members. Without specific conversations that help children make sense of the situation, the child cannot answer the question of who they are.

Children want to know how their family and life work. It is important to let your children know that you welcome a conversation on being an interfaith family. This is true even when the question is one that you don't have an answer to or that triggers a feeling of discomfort. It's fine to say that you don't know the answer, as long as you make sure to resume the conversation at a later point, when you have had time to think about or research the answer. Your children will get better information from you than from their peers. Help them anticipate which holidays they will be celebrating and where they will celebrate them, while at the same time talking about which holidays they will be able to enjoy with their relatives on both sides. Tell them who they are in terms of their religious identity. Encourage them to come to you when they feel confused. Think of these conversations as giving children a road map to their unique family.

CHAPTER 12

Fun and Games at the Jewish Community Center

It didn't take long after Gabbi was born for my wife to start thinking about where to send our daughter for childcare. To tell the truth, the thought caught me off guard. After all, "our baby" wasn't even a year old yet. I hadn't even considered that my little girl would have to spend time in some strange place without Bonnie or me to look after her.

Even though I was scared just thinking about it, I nonetheless wanted to help decide where our daughter would begin to socialize with other kids, get her first little bits of schooling, learn to share, eat her graham crackers, and make new friends. And, of course, where she would have her feelings hurt when another kid stole her pink plastic horse. Where she would skin her knees on the playgr . . . All right, stop. That's enough. I was reading too much into it. But still, it was an important decision.

So, Bonnie and I started looking at the different childcare centers around town. Some we had heard great things about (you know, the ones with a three-year waiting list), and some we had heard a few unflattering remarks. Then there was the

Jewish Community Center (JCC) and its Early Childhood Center. I was naturally a little concerned when Bonnie brought up the idea of enrolling our daughter there. Sure, it had a remarkable reputation. Still, I was a little apprehensive about sending Gabbi to a place where, as I thought, she would learn nothing but Hebrew. I wanted her to have a "normal" childcare experience.

"You will look into it with me, right?" Bonnie had asked.

"Honey, I don't know."

"Everyone says they have excellent teachers there."

"I know, but will she learn about stuff other than Israel?"

As it turned out, the JCC taught kids a lot about Israel and Judaism. They also taught myriad non-Jewish subjects. As we looked into it in depth, we found that the JCC had everything we were searching for in a childcare center: great teachers, a wonderful director and staff, a spacious playground for sunny days, a big gymnasium for rainy days, fun classrooms where the children could play and learn, and best of all, a warm, welcoming atmosphere. The decision became easy. Gabbi would begin her school career in the Bunny Room of the JCC's Early Childhood Center. Now I couldn't wait for her to start.

As time went on, my little girl became a big girl at the JCC. She was learning a lot. As it turned out, I was learning a lot, too. Year after year, we continued to register Gabbi at the JCC. Why? Because it offered so much more than I could have ever imagined.

One of the biggest reasons was that it gave us a sense of community. The JCC was not just for kids. We parents were also welcomed as part of the center. My wife and I got not only a feeling of belonging, but also a chance to be involved. Bonnie began serving on the board of the JCC. It was a great opportunity to have a say in our children's education. I got to volunteer at various functions, including fund-raisers, Shabbat dinners, and other holiday functions, and I've been known to serve ice cream at Family Fun Night. They actually expected me to scoop more than I ate. Where else could you find this much trust?

This sense of community did not stop there, either. The seniors in our area were extremely active at the JCC; they also participated in many of the Early Childhood Center's holiday parties and events. After a while, we got to know many wonderful and intriguing people of all generations and backgrounds. There was a special bond that we shared, as we were all part of this center.

The JCC's special events provided our family with an opportunity to meet other families with whom we have a lot in common. Many were part of an interfaith family, just as we were. It was reassuring to have friends who faced similar issues. However, as alike as some of our backgrounds were, there were many families who came from all over the world. We found it just as fun to develop friendships with families from Russia, Japan, Sweden, Israel, India, and other reaches of the globe. Even while most families at the JCC were Jewish, the center welcomed people of all faiths. Friendly and enlightening—what more could we ask for?

These functions also provided a much-needed chance to celebrate Judaism with our community. It was fun to call up friends and ask, "Are you going to the Sukkot dinner tomorrow night?" And while we taught Gabbi Judaism in the home, these functions reinforced her Jewish education by creating wonderful memories for her. In addition, during the day when she was in class, the teachers would read stories and create fun projects for whatever holiday was approaching. During Yom Kippur, for example, Gabbi learned all about Jonah and the whale and painted a picture of Jonah inside the whale's stomach. Every Friday, the kids celebrated Shabbat with a song leader and baked challah to take home for dinner.

For Gabbi, aspects of her Jewish culture and faith were now starting to click. One Friday afternoon as I picked Gabbi up at school, she began singing "Shabbat Shalom—Hey!" Later that evening, as Bonnie lit the candles, Gabbi began reciting the blessing. Bonnie and I exchanged a surprised look. Sure, we had said it on many Friday evenings before, but now, with the JCC reinforcing it at school, she was actually learning the Sabbath prayers at age one and a half.

I was struck by how beautiful it was that Gabbi had memorized these religious blessings. Then I thought, "This is it. She really is learning Judaism. Wow." Sure, we had given her a Hebrew name, but she didn't have to do anything for that. This was Gabbi taking an active role in her religious education. Hearing her recite the blessings was like watching a seed that we had planted when we decided to raise her Jewish bloom into a flower.

When Gabbi graduated from the JCC program, she continued to attend all the after-school functions with us and helped her little sister Molly navigate the Kangaroo Room. As a big sister should, she took charge in showing Molly all the ins and outs of being a JCC preschooler.

As an interfaith family raising our children Jewish, we were never quite sure if we were sending a consistent message to our kids. Did my being Christian confuse them? I'm sure it did, to a point. But while I continued to be a Protestant and taught my children about my religion, I would always find ways to reinforce their Judaism. This was one area where we found the JCC to be of the most benefit. The center's Early Childhood Program provided that sense of Jewish culture, community, religion, and life that other schools could not.

Part IV
CELEBRATING THE HOLIDAYS

CHAPTER 13

Teaching My Parents about Judaism

"*Gimmel*!" my dad shouted as he scooped up the pile of jelly beans in the center of the table. He was referring to the letter of the Hebrew alphabet on the dreidel that had just landed face up, meaning he had won. It was Hanukkah, and we had invited my parents over for our annual dinner and game of dreidel. In my family, we play with such fervor for jelly beans in addition to the usual chocolate coins called *gelt*.

We had just finished eating a wonderful meal of chicken, broccoli, and latkes (potato pancakes) with applesauce. Earlier, my parents had helped us light the menorah (the candelabrum of eight candles, plus one "helper" candle, that is lit during Hanukkah). My mom and dad even sang some of the traditional songs with us. While they didn't do any of the cooking, they did play with our two daughters, Gabbi and Molly, so we could prepare the meal.

In many Jewish homes, it is not unusual for the grandparents to help out with religious celebrations—unless, that is, they're not Jewish. I've had many years now to learn about Judaism from Bonnie. My mom and dad, on the other hand, began getting serious about learning more when our first daughter, Gabbi, was born. Before then, they had an interested, but limited knowledge of my wife's religion. The introduction of a grandchild into the family can have that effect. My parents are very loving and family-oriented. Fortunately for us, they were really excited about helping their grandchildren celebrate their holidays.

The first step that Bonnie and I took in bringing my parents into the fold was explaining each holiday to them. For example, we told them about Shabbat, why we eat apples and honey on Rosh Hashanah, and why Bonnie fasts on Yom Kippur. The first time I built a sukkah (hut for eating and sleeping in during the holiday of Sukkot), I explained to my dad why I just built this, in his words, "tool shed with a leaky roof." He was only trying to be funny. But, all kidding aside, my dad thought the whole tradition of inviting friends and family over for a special meal to be eaten under the stars was really "neat." It made me feel good that he took the time to ask about it and learn another aspect of the Jewish religion. Today, my parents know all about Sukkot and can speak intelligently about it with their grandchildren. I dare say, they know more about it than some of my Jewish friends who do not pay much attention to this holiday. I wouldn't call Mom and Dad experts, but at least they're knowledgeable. For instance, they probably couldn't tell a *lulav* from an *etrog* (two symbolic objects found in the sukkah), but at least they've seen them and know where they belong.

I think my parents enjoy learning as much as they can about their grandkids' religion. It helps them feel a lot more comfortable and welcome when they help our children celebrate their holidays. My mom and dad were just as much of a fixture at the Jewish Community Center preschool holiday functions as any other kid's grandparents. Granted, they often had to be reminded when a Jewish holiday was coming up (having holidays based on a lunar calendar doesn't help).

Of course, living in an interfaith family can have its advantages. It opens all sorts of windows to parts of society that you never knew existed. I know my life is richer for having met Bonnie and learned about Judaism. I try to pass these discoveries along to my parents, as well. I remember one day I was sitting around talking with my mom and dad about how lucky we were that all of our parents had been relatively accepting of our marriage. Many parents (of both religions) do not favor intermarriage. From a Jewish standpoint, one reason, I explained, is that many feel that it's harder to perpetuate their culture and religion if their members keep intermarrying. I don't think my mom and dad had ever looked at it that way.

Helping my parents understand their grandchildren's Judaism is not all about "on this holiday you sing this, and on this holiday you eat that." Living in the United States, my parents and I have always been in the majority. For the first time, I was able to show them a perspective that I had learned from a minority culture. Now, in my own way, I have become a part of that minority. And, like it or not (and they do), my parents have, as well.

OTHER VOICES

Holidays can be a particularly challenging time for families of different faiths, but they can also be a wonderful time to reach out to extended family. Each holiday on the Jewish calendar has its own special message that offers a unique opportunity to educate both Jews and non-Jews about Judaism in a warm and welcoming way.

Since many Jewish holidays are observed in the home, invite family and friends of other faiths to help prepare for and participate in the celebration. Ever since Karen and David were married, David's Jewish mother, Aviva, has invited Karen's Protestant family to the Passover seder. After a few years of participating, Aviva began inviting both Karen and her mother to help prepare the meal. The informal time spent preparing food together gives all three women the chance to share stories of family holidays and imagine together what Passover might be like with grandchildren present. The families also gather for Shabbat dinner on special occasions, such as on Karen and David's anniversary. While Karen's father doesn't feel comfortable leading the prayer over the wine (Kiddush), he shares his love and knowledge of fine wines by bringing new kosher wines to try at holiday celebrations.

Opportunities for learning and teaching about other religions through holidays often go both ways in interfaith families. Karen observes Advent by lighting a colored candle on a special table wreath during each of the four weeks preceding Christmas. She explains the tradition as being similar to the concept of the Hebrew month of Elul, a time for Jews to begin preparing themselves mentally and spiritually for the High Holiday season. Though the two holidays have quite different meanings, they share an emphasis on a period of preparation, supporting a common belief in the need to approach religious observances with thought and intentionality. After some years of working out the kinks in this approach, Karen and David now celebrate holidays with both sides of their family in a way that is comfortable and fun for everyone.

CHAPTER 14

Shabbat: The Holiday That Comes Every Week

Flashback:

It's 5:42 Friday evening. I'm in my car driving home from work, when all of a sudden I realize I've been singing for the last six minutes. I'm not singing to anything on the radio. No, I'm singing, "Shabbat Shalom, Hey! Shabbat Shalom, Hey!" Why am I singing this particular song?

Of all the Jewish holidays, I especially enjoy celebrating the most important one—Shabbat. This is the Jewish Sabbath, and it comes every Friday at sundown. After a week like the one I've just had, it's a welcome respite. Every single day we rushed to work, preschool, doctor appointments, a softball game, and a birthday party at Chuck E. Cheese. Now, it's time to slow down and enjoy a nice dinner with the family. In the old days, my grandparents used to observe the Christian Sabbath on Sunday in a similar fashion. For them, it was a day to rest. Stores were closed; nobody rushed off to a hockey game. In addition, the dinner played a big role, in gathering the family to the table to say a prayer and be together. It's too bad that practice is no longer as common as it used to be.

At 5:54, I pull my car into the garage. Dog-tired, I enter through the laundry room and BAM! I'm hit on both legs by my two little cuties, who have wrapped their arms around me while yelling, "Daddy's home!" Carrying the two of them, seated on both of my feet, I walk like Frankenstein into the kitchen to greet Bonnie. She's already set out the Shabbat candles and the Kiddush cup of wine on the table. The challah is just coming out of the oven. The house smells great. I feel a little bit like Fred Flintstone home from a day at the quarry—only Fred never had to help cook. For Shabbat dinner, we often grill. I'm pretty good at cooking with fire. Anytime there's an element of danger involved in food preparation, I'm there. It must be a tribal instinct.

It's 6:20 and the chicken is done (a little burned, but done). It sits on the platter, smoldering and waiting for us to dig in. But first, we must say the blessings. According to Jewish law, we're supposed to wait until sundown. Unfortunately, sundown for us in Michigan is on the western edge of the eastern time zone. In the summer, we'd have to wait until after 9:00 p.m. Our girls' bedtime is at 8:30, so we start early.

The ritual begins with Gabbi doling out yarmulkes to everyone, based on their favorite color. Then, Bonnie and Gabbi light the candles and recite the blessing over the Sabbath lights. It's great to hear my daughter use Hebrew. Molly, who has big brown eyes that get even bigger with the candlelight, takes it all in.

After each blessing tonight, we make sure to say the prayer in English, as well. We feel strongly that the kids should know what the prayer means, instead of simply rattling off the Hebrew. Being Protestant and not growing up around Hebrew, I also enjoy the translation. When I first learned the Hebrew blessings a few years back, I had no idea what they meant. Then, when

I heard them in English, I realized that they were very similar in nature to the prayer my father recites at Christmas dinner. Saying the prayers in English makes our family ritual feel more inclusive and accessible for me.

Since our daughters were born, we've recited the blessing over the children—first in Hebrew, then in English. "May God make you as Sarah, Rebekah, Rachel, and Leah."

"Sarah who, Daddy?" Molly asks. "Gabbi's friend, Sarah Starman?" Bonnie and I exchange a humorous look and then proceed to tell her about the four matriarchs of Jewish history.

I admit that I needed a little brushing up on that part of history, too. My parents never said this type of blessing over my siblings and me. So, before the first time we recited the prayer, Bonnie gave me an overview of who the four matriarchs were. The fact that this is a new concept for me and that I'm asking my daughters to emulate Jewish women does not bother me. If I look in the Bible of my youth, I'd find these women. Besides, the four matriarchs are not bad examples to follow.

Next, I say the blessing over the wine. We raise the antique Kiddush cup and drink from it. For the kids' benefit, it's filled with kosher grape juice. Bonnie holds the cup tightly for the girls when they drink, so that it's not dropped. After all, this cup belonged to her grandmother. Every time I drink out of it, I feel in awe of the tradition behind it. In my mind, I picture Bonnie's *bubba* as a young mother and my father-in-law as a boy. I picture her also holding the cup firmly in her strong hands, preventing him from dropping it to the floor, preserving it for future generations. "Thanks, Bubba," I think to myself.

Finally, we say Hamotzi, the blessing over the challah. It's about time, too. Molly, for the last ten minutes, has said nothing but "hallaaaah, hallaaaah, hallaaaah" over and over again. Of course, she's finished her piece before I've even said the word *Baruch.*

When we sit down at the table to enjoy a good meal (I'm too relaxed to remember what time it is), I appreciate the fact that we're all here together. I start to remember for the first time since last Friday that this is what Shabbat is all about—thanking God. We thank God for all that God has given us. We thank God for our health and the gift that we can share this moment on a nice, quiet Friday evening. Maybe the food's not perfect, but the time together certainly is.

"Strange isn't it?" I think to myself. When Bonnie and I were first married, she told me that she would like to have a nice Shabbat dinner now and then. And every once and a while, we did. Now that we have two daughters, we've been making every effort to see that they learn about Judaism and what it means to be Jewish. My mind starts counting the weeks backward a few months. Then it strikes me. Without realizing what we were doing, we had been observing Shabbat every Friday night as far back as I could remember. Not bad for a couple who originally wanted to just fit it in when we could. Never in my wildest dreams did I imagine that I'd look forward every week to a Shabbat dinner. After a crazy week, I am grateful for this moment to catch my breath, count my blessings, and spend time with my family.

Fast-forward:

It's 7:45 p.m., and Molly drives home from field hockey practice, locks her car in the driveway, and enters the house. "Helloooooo. I'm hoooooooome!" The kitchen smells great. Bonnie has already set out the challah and the Kiddush cup.

I bring in the burnt chicken from the grill. "Hi, Mol. How was practice?"

"Good. I'm dog-tired, though."

At 7:50 p.m., Gabbi enters the house, looking sluggish from her English exam and lengthy rehearsal with her college acting group. "I'm hooooooooome."

"Hi Gabbi. How'd it go?"

"Good. I think."

"I'm sure you'll do fine. Ready for Shabbat?"

OTHER VOICES

Parents who are not Jewish often wonder what role they can play in reinforcing the decision to raise the children within Judaism. Children need both of their parents to nurture and support a religious identity decision. Whereas the Jewish parent often serves as an ambassador into Jewish life and rituals, the role of the parent from another faith background is equally important.

Rick, a Christian dad, was at home alone with his two young children one Friday evening. His Jewish wife, Rachel, a nurse, unexpectedly had to work an extra shift. Rick realized that his kids would still expect to do their special shared Shabbat family rituals—the lighting of the candles, the grape juice, and the challah, for which Rachel always took the lead role. So Rick set out the challah and grape juice and hunted around, unsuccessfully, for the Shabbat candles and candlesticks. Unable to reach Rachel on the phone, he decided instead to use birthday candles for the Shabbat blessings and, not having any other candlesticks to use, inserted them into the challah and poured out a cup of grape juice for each child. He and the children joyously sang the Shabbat blessings together. Responding to the new twist of the birthday candles in the challah, each child made a wish and promptly blew out the candles.

When Rachel came home from work later that evening, she thanked Rick for maintaining the weekly ritual for their children in her absence. Rick told her how much he had enjoyed helping the kids have Shabbat. When he told her about the "new tradition" he had begun, she laughed and suggested that they add a "Shabbat wish" to the weekly moments of blessing. On future Friday nights, Rick and Rachel went back to using their

Shabbat candles and candlesticks and let the candles glow until they burned down, but they now incorporated the ritual of a "Shabbat wish" into the candlelighting ceremony. Rick felt great that he had added something original to their family's celebration of Shabbat. With his children at his side, Rick was following through on his desire to be a part of, not apart from, his family's celebration of Jewish life.

CHAPTER 15

The High Holidays: A Time for Both of Us to Learn

September for many Christians in the United States brings thoughts of "back to school," football games, and apple cider. Bonnie experiences this too, but to her, September means something much more significant. It is time for the Jewish High Holidays of Rosh Hashanah and Yom Kippur. This is a time to be with her family, go to services, dip apples in honey, and atone for sins of the past year.

Because of all that goes on at this time of year, both partners may be experiencing warm, fuzzy feelings, but for different reasons. I certainly don't equate the start of the football season with the importance of the High Holidays, but I do feel it is necessary for my wife to realize that her Protestant spouse did not grow up with the same experiences. Fortunately for me, Bonnie has always been understanding and eased me into the Jewish experience at a pace that was comfortable for me. Important note to the Christian partner reading this: Don't think for a minute that I'm going to sit here and tell you that your Jewish spouse has to do all the accommodating. You should consider putting down your caramel apple, turning off the game on the TV, and trying just as hard to understand the significance of the season for him or her.

The first time I experienced the High Holidays with my wife was after we were engaged, and I wasn't sure what to think. We went to her dad's house for Rosh Hashanah. I loved being with all of her family. I also loved the tasty food that was served nonstop for two days. Going to temple, though, was a different story. It was my first time *ever* in a synagogue. It's not like going to a different church, where a few minor details are changed around but otherwise it's all basically the same. At my in-laws' temple, not only was it a foreign holiday for me, but there was a lot of Hebrew used in the service. I didn't know what was going on. The fact that I had to sit there for three hours did not help my restlessness. Most Protestant services are only one hour long, and they're in English. Even though Bonnie did her best to explain what was happening and what some of the Hebrew meant, and even though Bonnie's parents tried to make me feel as welcome as possible in their synagogue, I felt lost.

After temple, we went back to Bonnie's parents' house, where Bonnie helped me learn more about her holiday. She explained the meaning of the Torah portion read that day. We dipped apples in honey "for a sweet new year." Even though my wife was surrounded by friends and family, I was really happy that she spent extra time with me that day. The Christian partner can have feelings of being alone or isolated on Rosh Hashanah. A little hand-holding can go a long way.

Eight days after Rosh Hashanah comes Yom Kippur. To a Christian, this can feel like a double whammy—first the Jewish New Year, and then the Day of Atonement. Rosh Hashanah is festive and happy, but Yom Kippur has a serious and somber aspect to it. Protestants don't have anything like this holiday. Catholics have confession, but not a whole day devoted to atoning, praying, and fasting.

We had talked about Yom Kippur in advance so that there would be no surprises. This kind of advance preparation is very important for interfaith couples. The fewer surprises, the better. I did not fast but felt it was important for me to respect my wife's situation. (Note to Christians: Don't eat a big bowl of Cheerios in front of your spouse on this day. Try to do your eating discreetly and out of sight.) While Bonnie did not expect me to fast along with her, she was still unaccustomed to being around someone who was eating. (Note to Jews: Remember that your partner, if he is not fasting with you, will still need nourishment. Don't take it as a lack of respect if he eats. Just try to be someplace else if it makes your stomach growl like Godzilla with a bellyache.)

Once again, I went to services with Bonnie—actually, twice that day. Being at the temple was not my idea of fun. Where I really enjoyed myself was watching and admiring my wife during this most holy day for her. I was not about to complain. This was my wife's day, and I would see her through it. To my great surprise, she slipped me a protein bar during the service and told me to go take a break outside. I was floored. I was speechless. About the only thing I could do was give her a peck on the cheek and head for the door. When I came back ten minutes later, she had a big smile on her face. I think it was caused by a combination of giving me pleasure and knowing that it would soon be time to break the fast.

At first, I didn't think my wife could fast all day. Bonnie loves food. She is a "foodie." So I didn't know how seriously she would take the fasting. I was sure she wouldn't make it. But I learned a lot that day. I developed a newfound respect for her and her religious convictions. Not only did she make it, but she also never complained.

Yom Kippur can feel like a long holiday, but you're rewarded with a big spread of food at the end. The most significant thing we learned was that it is important to be respectful of each other's feelings on this day. Bonnie's thoughtfulness and validation of my attempt to support her had a positive impact on my overall experience. Giving each other the support to make it through strengthened our relationship that much more.

In short, when it comes to the High Holidays, Jewish partners can help by remembering that their Christian partners may have feelings of insecurity or of not fitting in with your family or temple. Sometimes they might just be plain ignorant of your traditions, feelings, and experiences. Don't forget to help guide them. It'll pay off in the long run.

Each couple needs to decide whether they will accompany each other to their respective houses of worship. This of course gets more complicated when children arrive. In our case, Bonnie and I decided that I would go with the girls and her to temple on their holidays, and they would travel with me to church on mine. We felt this was extremely helpful in learning about each other's religions—especially when it came to teaching our children. Just as important, it is a show of support and love for each other. As a couple, we constantly work to show our spouse that his or her faith is important. As parents, we also need to send the right message. Just because Dad is Christian, it doesn't mean that he doesn't care about his family's Jewish faith. That's why he comes to temple with us. Along the same lines, Mom and the children can show Dad that they care by going to church with him on special occasions.

Bonnie and I had been cautious when it came to taking the

kids to my church. At an early age, we could see how it might be confusing for them. To prevent that, we made sure to have them accompany me only once in a while—Christmas Eve most notably. We also emphasized that they are Jewish and were there only to help me with my celebration. This is Dad's church; they go to a synagogue.

Today, I am a fixture at the temple with my family. When the kids come along with me to church, they enjoy the special event. Bonnie and I have set a pattern that is predictable for our children. They have been well versed in our game plan and know what to expect. Consistency is the key. Over time, thanks to Bonnie's help, I've found myself feeling more and more comfortable with her holidays. I have learned the rituals of the different services. I have made friends at the temple. I have even learned some Hebrew. Every year I see how much more I can follow along in the prayer book by improving my recognition of the Hebrew letters and words. I now look forward to Rosh Hashanah and Yom Kippur. I actually get a warm, fuzzy feeling over these holidays. After all these years of marriage, it's getting to be that September can't roll around without me breaking out my football, fall clothes, and shofar.

OTHER VOICES

While making the decision to be a Jewish family means a great deal of adjustment for the partner of another faith, it also means adjustment and accommodation from the Jewish partner. The High Holidays are a time when that reality comes into especially sharp focus, as couples encounter the mood of the season and the challenges in sharing unfamiliar worship and other rituals.

Dana was used to spending the whole day of Yom Kippur in synagogue. Before they had children, Jack, a Methodist, would treat the day like almost any other, including going to work when it fell on a weekday. Dana felt abandoned and alone on what she considered one of the most important days of the year, but she never said anything, as she did not want to impose her observance on Jack. When their oldest child reached preschool age, Dana asked Jack to stay home from work so that she could spend the day in synagogue and not have to leave their child with babysitters on a day that should be spent differently. Jack readily agreed, and as the kids got older and attended the synagogue's children's programs, he began to attend the morning services with Dana. He had, in fact, been willing to do so all along, but since Dana never raised the matter, Jack saw no reason to do so.

Dana was surprised at how much it mattered to her that her partner was, on some level, sharing the solemnity of the day, even if it was not his own holiday. Jack's desire to be a caring and supportive partner made all the difference. And it turned out that the themes of the day resonated with Jack in a meaningful, even profound way. He appreciated the fact that though the day is, in so many ways, God centered, its goals are humanistic, inspiring worshippers to grow and become more than they had been. Jack appreciated that the images of God were accessible, if somewhat different than he was accustomed to finding at a prayer service. The notion of *t'shuvah*—repentance and return— was not only familiar, but was, for Jack, an essential religious teaching. The approach was new but echoed values that he had held closely throughout his life. He was intrigued by the notion of responsibility for resolving one's relationships with others as grounded in the relationship with God, and he appreciated the opportunity for self-reflection that Yom Kippur provided. While Jack chose not to fast and attended only the morning service on Yom Kippur, the day became one of important spiritual growth for both Dana and Jack, as well as a valuable shared experience.

CHAPTER 16

Sukkot? Never Heard of It

I have to admit I never knew that a holiday called Sukkot existed until I met Bonnie. I'd be surprised if 10 percent of the non-Jewish population of our hometown of Ann Arbor had heard of it either. It's not a holiday that gets a lot of press. This is really a shame, because I have found it to be one of the most enjoyable holidays of either religion. It is a time to remember the Jews who wandered the desert for forty years, a time to celebrate the harvest, a time to be grateful for all our blessings, and a time to spend with family and friends.

The year 1999 was a big one for my family. Not only was our second daughter born, but we also moved into a new house. Coincidentally, we happened to move in right before Sukkot. After getting the majority of boxes emptied and put away, I came across our disassembled sukkah. A sukkah is a temporary structure that Jewish families erect in their backyards during Sukkot to remind them of the portable huts the Jews lived in while they were wandering in the desert. Often they are built of wood, though prefab *sukkot* made of metal piping are becoming popular, and they are decorated with all sorts of items, including gourds, cornstalks, and paper chains.

No Sukkot celebration is complete without a *lulav* and *etrog*. The *lulav* is made up of three branches that are placed together in a holder—one of palm, one of willow, and one of myrtle. An *etrog* is a citron, which is a fruit, like a big aromatic lemon. (Ironically, the only other time I've ever heard of a citron was when my aunt Alice baked some into her delicious Christmas bread that she used to send us every December.) After reciting a special Sukkot blessing, each person takes a turn holding the *lulav* and *etrog* together, shaking them in each direction. Because the *lulav* and *etrog* are made of real plants, you need to order fresh sets each year from your synagogue.

We had bought this particular sukkah kit (lumber, brackets, screws, and all) at a temple fund-raiser a few years earlier. As I took inventory of the different pieces, I was delighted that it was almost time to put it up. This meant, for the time being, that I wouldn't have to find a place to store it in our already overstuffed garage.

When the first day of Sukkot arrived, I dragged all the parts to the backyard. It took me only an hour and ten minutes to raise the structure. Over the years, I have gotten this process down to a science. I'm like an Indy pit crew with my power drill. Sometimes my father-in-law is in town to help me (although he just holds the bag of screws). Then we can build it in under an hour. You should see the sparks fly—we're good!

I was just putting the finishing touches on our sukkah when my next-door neighbor stopped over to talk. He had a wary look on his face. He was curious about this "shed" that I was building that took up a majority of our small backyard. He was greatly relieved when I told him about my wife's holiday and that the sukkah would be coming down at the end of Sukkot. Once I told him about the festival, he didn't care how long it was up. He thought it was nice to have something different going on in the neighborhood.

One of my favorite things about Sukkot is that it is a time to celebrate with neighbors, friends, and family. It is a tradition to invite guests to join in a holiday meal in the sukkah. Bonnie and I put a table and chairs in the sukkah, invite our friends over, and have meals in it. It takes backyard barbecuing to a whole new level. When our friends come over, we cook tasty dishes, the kids and their friends make decorations, and once the kids are in bed, the grown-ups sit in the sukkah for hours talking. It's refreshing to be with company in a different environment, where the TV is off and the phone is left in the house. You'd be amazed at what this does for the quality of conversation.

Another great part of Sukkot is the requirement that the roof of the sukkah be covered with branches, palms, or leaves, so that a certain percentage of the sky is visible. It must be open enough so you can see the stars at night. I've always loved to camp, and I'm still hoping to get Gabbi and Molly to camp out there with me one of these years. Sure, we're not in the woods or mountains— it's just our backyard. However, there's something rewarding in being able to teach my daughters about their holidays. To have fun while doing it is a bonus. And in the morning, when my back is sore, I can take a long hot shower.

Our lives can get pretty routine at times. Why not take the opportunity to do something different and build a sukkah? If ever there were a chance to do the out-of-the-ordinary, a chance to turn your backyard into a magical place, this would be it.

Sukkot is a fun holiday. I'm very lucky to be able to take advantage of this time with my wife and kids. When Dad starts building the sukkah, it's like an electrical charge hits Gabbi and Molly. Many of our Jewish friends do not build a sukkah because it wasn't a part of their childhood experiences. When they come over for dinner in our sukkah, they laugh at how it took a Protestant to get them to celebrate the holiday in the proper way. I'm proud that I can help my kids know that this week of Sukkot is special. This week, our family will be doing things differently around the house. This week, they will learn a little more about their Jewish heritage.

OTHER VOICES

For one interfaith couple, Hannah and Mark, Sukkot is their children's favorite holiday. The weekend before Sukkot begins, uncles and cousins from both sides of the family come together to build the sukkah. Since Sukkot comes at the beginning of the school year, the family creates an informal invitation that is given to every student and teacher in the children's class, as well as other friends, family, and neighbors. For Hannah and Mark, Sukkot is a wonderful opportunity to get to know new people and renew old friendships. Anyone and everyone is welcome to an open-house afternoon of socializing and enjoying the bounty of the fall harvest foods such as nuts, apple cider, popcorn, and garden vegetables. Guests are also invited to bring something to help decorate the sukkah, such as gourds, flowers and herbs, popcorn strings, or peppers.

Sukkot is also known as the "Season of Our Joy" and as such is often compared to a Jewish Thanksgiving. At the end of their Sukkot open-house afternoon, Hannah, Mark and their children lead their guests in the holiday blessings, and then each mentions something for which they are thankful. Hannah notes that she always takes the opportunity to welcome everyone and offer thanks for friends and family, who bring richness and diversity to their lives. At the end of the day, the family hosts a potluck meal in the sukkah, including homemade soup and bread prepared by Hannah, her mother, and Mark's sister. The beautifully adorned sukkah remains throughout the week, and each child has the opportunity to invite one special friend and his or her family to a more intimate dinner in the sukkah on another evening of the festival. In this way, the family has created a Sukkot celebration that is welcoming and comfortable for all of their friends and relatives. The celebration of Sukkot has become, for this family, a way to bridge differences and be inclusive.

CHAPTER 17

Will Santa Bring Me Presents Even If I'm Jewish?

Ahhh, yes. The December dilemma. It's something we parents in interfaith families look forward to all year. The confusion. The doubt. The inconsistency. It doesn't have to be this way, though. There are workable solutions. With a little effort and perseverance, you can get through the season with your family and sanity still intact.

My wife and I have striven hard for answers that fit our particular situation. Every family will have unique issues to face. There is no single correct way to resolve this dilemma, and the emphasis here is on the plurality of the word "solutions."

However you decide to handle it, the earlier you begin working out how your family will deal with the Christmas and Hanukkah season, the better. Bonnie and I started while we were engaged. We suddenly realized that yes, one day we would have children. What to do? We had no clue. We just knew that it was better to go into family life with a game plan. We felt that if we waited to figure it out after our children were born, we would be susceptible to disaster.

When Bonnie and I decided that we were going to raise

our children as Jews, it clearly meant that we were not going to raise our kids in both religions. At the same time, we knew that whatever plan we came up with would have to be flexible. We hadn't had children yet, so we couldn't possibly know what it would be like when the reality hit us. We had to create a plan that allowed for minor adjustments. It would have to be like the Constitution of the United States—the door should always be open for change under the right circumstances. The important thing was to make sure we were consistent and that the kids knew they were Jewish and therefore celebrated Hanukkah.

Having already decided to raise the kids Jewish, we knew they would celebrate Hanukkah, and I would *help* them celebrate their holiday. That was the easy part. But I am Christian and still celebrate Christmas. Christmas is an important holiday for me, and I wanted our children to learn about my holidays. In addition, Christmas was a time to be with my parents and my siblings, both of whom are married and have children. We are a close family and all live in the same town. We always get together for the holidays. How would my children react if they had to sit still and watch their cousins open a bunch of presents from Santa? And it's not just the presents. The spirit of the holiday is everywhere during the Christmas season. There are trees to be decorated, cookies to bake, and lights to be strung. Santa's jolly pink face is everywhere—even on your can of Coke. These are all fun things that I grew up with and was not about to give up, even if American marketing would let me. So we decided that Bonnie and the kids would *help* me celebrate my holidays. They would wind up learning about Christmas and what Christmas means to me. But as Jews, they would understand that they were only assisting Daddy with *his* celebration.

In 1996, Gabbi was born. Three and a half years later, Molly came into our world. It was easy when Gabbi was an infant—she didn't ask questions. All we had to do was stick to our plan. But by the time Molly was born, Gabbi had started to ask *lots* of questions.

"Who in our family is Jewish? Which grandparents are Christian?" She was starting to categorize things. It's cool, she does this with her stuffed animals: "These three are bears, these two are froggies," and so on. A completely age-appropriate activity.

But then she started to ask, "Does Daddy celebrate Hanukkah? Do I get Hanukkah *and* Christmas presents? Will Santa bring me presents even if I'm Jewish?"

We had been afraid something like this would happen. Gabbi started putting two and two together in an appropriate three-year-old way and realized that it's the Christians—not the Jews—who celebrate this holiday with the tree and Santa. This led to one big anxiety attack that she wasn't going to get *any* presents. We calmed her fears by reminding her of all the nice Hanukkah presents that she was going to get. We also explained that it's much more important to give than to receive and that both holidays are about giving.

We didn't want to put too much emphasis on the gift aspect. As our daughters have gotten older, we've been able to explain to them that the holidays are not centered on presents, but rather are to celebrate special events that took place a long time ago. We have made sure to tell the story of Hanukkah. The girls know all about Judah Maccabee and the miracle of the oil that burned for eight days. In addition, in religious school they have learned about the importance of religious freedom that the Hanukkah story relates.

Likewise, we have not shied away from teaching Gabbi and

Molly about why my side of the family and I celebrate Christmas. We want them to know that it isn't because of Santa Claus; it is about the birth of Jesus. They understand the story and that my Christian beliefs are not theirs. As a result, their assisting me (and their subsequent interest) has chiefly been focused on the secular American traditions of Christmas. Bonnie and I still go to great pains to make sure they know that even the nonreligious aspects of my holiday are not a part of their faith. But I do enjoy their help.

Once we were sure that they understood the ground rules, we didn't want our kids to focus on the differences in our family. Instead, Bonnie and I have tried to nurture a sense of identity for our children that they could be proud of, while realizing that their religion and culture are just part of who they are. This, we believe, is the most important part. They are a lot of things: they are girls, they have brown eyes, Gabbi likes to sing and act, Molly likes to laugh at the dog, and, yes, they are Jewish. Dad is tall, he has green eyes, and he is Christian. Mom is pretty, she likes chocolate, and she is Jewish.

The next obstacle we had to overcome was keeping a consistent approach to the holidays. At first, my Protestant parents kept asking us what kind of gift, if any, to give the girls on Christmas morning. Christmas or Hanukkah presents? We had to admit, we were slightly unprepared for the question. The gifts had never had an identifying label attached to them. But then again, the girls had never asked—until now. This is why we had made our plan flexible. We knew we'd have to adapt to the unexpected.

After we discussed it for a few days, we finally decided how we'd explain things to our kids. Hanukkah was simple; the kids get Hanukkah presents. Christmas, which we celebrate at my parents' house, was more complicated. We decided to tell Gabbi and Molly, "Santa brings you a couple of late Hanukkah presents on Christmas, because he knows you're Jewish." What we've now worked out is that my parents and in-laws give the major gifts to our daughters on Hanukkah. Meanwhile, my parents save one or two smaller Hanukkah presents for Christmas morning. This seems to work well for us. The message to the girls that they are Jewish is consistently reinforced, but they're not excluded from the activities during my holiday. It's also important that my parents, who love to give presents, are not denied their pleasure on Christmas morning either.

Remembering how we explained it to my parents, we said it to the girls similarly like this: It's like going to someone else's birthday party. It's not *your* birthday that's being celebrated. You're there to help the birthday girl celebrate *her* birthday. But it doesn't mean you're not allowed to have fun, too. And when their grandparents give them a little something on Christmas morning, it's like getting a goodie bag at a birthday party, a treat for helping to celebrate that day.

While working through this not-so-simple problem, both Bonnie and I realized we were uncomfortable with other solutions and ways to phrase things to our children. Early on, Bonnie felt that it just wasn't right to celebrate Christmas at all with the kids. However, I wanted to share with the girls some of the joy and special feelings that I had from my childhood. There were emotions that we both felt that the other one couldn't possibly know. We had to make some tough decisions. Yes, there is a tree in our house, but it is *my* tree. Bonnie and the girls only *help* me decorate it. We do everything we can to keep it in a different room from the Hanukkah decorations. Of course, the separation is much easier on the years that the two holidays don't fall during the same week. My wife and daughters also attend church with me on Christmas Eve. We join up with my parents, siblings, and all the little cousins. This is another way for Bonnie and the girls to *help* me celebrate my holiday.

At first, we made a conscious effort to separate the two holidays as much as possible and identify who celebrated what. As time went on, though, handling the holidays has become more second nature to us. However, there's always that lingering thought in the backs of our minds, "Are we confusing our children?" Fortunately, Bonnie's stepmother offered us a refreshing bit of wisdom. She said, "One day out of the year isn't going to make or break their Jewish identity. It's how you raise your kids as Jews the other 364 days that counts."

In the end, we knew we were creating an interfaith family and would have to approach the holidays from a different angle than same-faith marriages. We are both comfortable with what we've decided. It may not work for everyone, but it fits our family nicely. In the years to come, I'm sure we'll have to face more surprises and twists. However, we have a solid foundation on which to build. We'll be ready.

OTHER VOICES

Jeff and Suzanne knew that the magic of Santa Claus mattered to Suzanne's Methodist parents, who wanted to pass along their many family Christmas traditions to all their grandchildren, including three-year-old grandson Sam, who was being raised within Judaism. Suzanne's mom was especially concerned that Sam might "spoil the magic" for his other young cousins if Sam did not believe that Santa delivered everyone's holiday presents.

Jeff and Suzanne created a strategy in which they told Sam that he would receive most of his presents during his holiday, Hanukkah, but that Santa knew Sam was Jewish and would include a Hanukkah present for him when Santa brought Christmas presents to Grandma's house for his Christian cousins. They shared their strategy with Suzanne's parents, who agreed to cooperate. Neither Suzanne nor Jeff saw the need to discuss it with Jeff's parents.

"Santa will be bringing me Hanukkah presents this year!" three-year-old Sam announced to his somewhat surprised Jewish grandmother as she tucked him into bed. Afterward, she asked Jeff and Suzanne about the comment, wondering how she should have responded. Jeff and Suzanne then shared their "Christmas strategy" with Jeff's parents. Jeff's parents were able to see the bigger picture of their young grandson's Jewish identity and managed not to "freak out" at the mention of Santa. Jeff's mom acknowledged that Sam clearly knew he was Jewish and felt joy in the Jewish rituals Suzanne and Jeff created in their home. Suzanne shared that her parents try to reinforce their grandson's Jewish identity as they are able but are very grateful that Sam is a part of some of her family's traditions as well. Jeff's parents understood that Suzanne's parents needed a way to share their holiday traditions with Sam.

Jeff and Suzanne now share their strategies on a range of issues with both sets of grandparents, and it has helped tremendously.

CHAPTER 18

Eggs and Plagues: Easter/Passover Issues

Spring in Michigan is always a welcome sight—just ask anyone who has ever spent a winter here. So when the snow melts and the crocuses bloom, everyone tends to get a little giddy. "Whadaya mean I can't wear shorts? It's fifty-two degrees. It's hot out!" Yes, people are excited. Of course, in my interfaith family, we have an extra reason to be elated. It's the season for Easter and Passover.

My wife and I each have fond memories of our holidays. For Bonnie, it's *matzah brei* (eggs and unleavened bread fried up in a pan) and getting together with her cousins for Passover. For me, it's Easter eggs and Disney World for spring break with my family. To this day, just the smell of vinegar (used in the dye) reminds me of the brightly colored eggs that the Easter Bunny hid for us. Like Christmas and Hanukkah, Easter and Passover can also evoke strong emotions in interfaith families.

Instead of letting these feelings be a source of strife for us, we decided to make them a springboard for embarking on a whole new set of experiences. We did not want to deny one of us our traditions by trying to pick which holiday would be celebrated in our household. As with our December dilemma, Bonnie and I decided that we would each "help" the other celebrate his or her holiday. We do this for other holidays. In that respect, Easter and Passover are no different.

One of the most important aspects of these two holidays, for both of us, is being with our families. My wife must be with her family for Passover or it just isn't the same. The big gathering of her parents, aunt, uncle, and cousins (and now their kids) is an annual happy occasion—even if it reaches the decibel level of a 747. We all get together in Boston for at least one of the two seders (Passover meals). We learn about Moses and the Pharaoh, the Ten Plagues, and the significance of the Passover food. There's lots of singing and lots to eat. (The food is delicious, but too much matzah gives me lead-belly.)

For my family, on Easter it is also important to be together. As kids, my brother, sister, and I used to dye Easter eggs on Saturday night. The morning of Easter Sunday, we'd wake up and scurry around the house looking for hidden eggs to put in our Easter baskets. As we grew older, we started to spend our spring-break vacation in Disney World. Because this break always occurred over Good Friday and Easter, it became a tradition to enjoy our holiday with Mickey. Today, my whole family, nuclear and extended, makes the trip to Florida. Like my wife and her side of the family, it just wouldn't feel right spending the holiday any other way.

There are many customs associated with these two holidays. However, the religious aspects of Easter and Passover are not to be ignored. Bonnie usually accompanies me to the Easter church service. I once asked her if all the talk of Jesus made her feel uncomfortable. She replied that as foreign as it was, she still viewed it as an educational experience. She said that going to church with me gave her an opportunity to learn more about my faith and background. Because we're on the road for Easter, I never quite know what to expect in a different congregation from my hometown. I'm always afraid that the minister will say something that might offend my wife. I don't know exactly what that would be; yet I still worry. Fortunately, my fears have not even remotely come true.

As Bonnie learns from my Easter experience, I, too, enjoy taking in the Passover scene. My first seder with her was on the campus of the University of Michigan, while we were dating. We went to a house with a bunch of friends, where our host proclaimed that putting on this seder made for a lot of happy mothers back home. Because we were students, we did a lot more eating and talking than anything. We skipped over quite a bit of the haggadah, the book containing the prayers, songs, and story of Passover. I was not intimidated in this setting, but I worried, how would it be when I experienced my first Passover with her big family at a "real" seder?

My wife has a wonderful family, but I worried about fitting in and not sticking out like a sore thumb at the dinner table. True to form though, they went out of their way to make sure I *didn't* feel uncomfortable. I was assigned duties around the kitchen just like everyone else. I can proudly say that I helped grate the horseradish for the Passover plate. (Each food on the plate is symbolic in some way. Horseradish symbolizes the bitterness of slavery the Jews experienced in Egypt.) However, I did feel out of place when passages were read in Hebrew or, even worse, sung in Hebrew! Not knowing the language is bad enough, let alone not knowing the tune. What was reassuring for me was feeling that everyone there *wanted* me to be a part of the family.

The first couple of years spending Passover with Bonnie's

family were a huge learning experience for me. There's a part of the seder when the leader of the service breaks a piece of matzah called the *afikoman*. In some families, the kids hide the *afikoman* and hold it for ransom. In Bonnie's family, sometimes the leader will hide it in the room and make the kids hunt for it. Now this I could relate to!

Over the years, I've gotten to know the different prayers, songs, and symbolisms of Passover. I've found that I can make the holiday as easy or as difficult as I want it to be. I've chosen to make it an experience from which I can absorb a lot about my wife's religion. As we learn more about each other's holidays, we, as parents, are better prepared to impart to our children the meaning of Dad's Easter and the traditions of their own Passover.

Part V

MEETING MY OWN NEEDS

CHAPTER 19

If I Can't Play Santa Claus, at Least I Can Be the Tooth Fairy

When Gabbi was five, she lost her first tooth. Actually, it was her first two teeth. They were getting crowded out by two newly erupted adult teeth and needed to be pulled. The dentist was having a two-for-one sale, so we yanked them.

After the tears were dried and the Popsicles slurped, I suddenly and delightedly realized, "Hey, the Tooth Fairy's got to come tonight." I had to be ready. So I explained to Gabbi how the whole thing works. "You put your teeth into this little box and put it under your pillow. While you're sleeping, the Tooth Fairy will come into your room and exchange the teeth for money."

Together, Gabbi and I put the teeth into the special silver box my mother gave her. We carefully hid it under her pillow as I tucked her in. Later that night, while she slept, I tiptoed into the room, searched for the box, finally found it underneath her Pooh Bear, took the teeth out, put the cash in, and crept out the door, banging my ankle on the dollhouse and nearly ruining the whole effort. As I closed the door and stood there in the hallway with Bonnie, a big grin came over my face.

"You know," I said, "this is a major milestone for us, as parents.

It's our first time playing Tooth Fairy. It's just like playing Santa Claus—all the make-believe and sneaking around at night."

Then, as soon as it had come, my smile went away. "Oh, wait a minute. I don't get to play Santa Claus," I thought sadly. I observe the Christmas holiday, not Hanukkah. My wife and daughters celebrate Hanukkah, not Christmas. So I don't get to be Santa Claus.

After experiencing the fun of being the Tooth Fairy (no, I didn't dress up in a tutu), it dawned on me that I had been denied the opportunity to play Santa for my kids. They don't celebrate Christmas, so I've always given them Hanukkah presents during the eight days of the holiday. There really isn't a "Hanukkah Harry" to dress up as, so the thrill of delivering presents in the middle of the night has been missing since my children were born.

However, the arrangement in our family, I reminded myself, works. I wouldn't want to change a thing—especially not just so I can fill stockings at midnight. Upon further reflection, I felt pretty happy about the course Bonnie and I had set for our family. Fortunately, I could now get my stealthy magical-character fix from playing the role of the Tooth Fairy.

As the only Christian in our family, I've come to realize that I have certain needs, too. It's always a tricky line to walk in making sure that I fulfill those needs and not undermine what my wife and I have worked so hard to achieve for our family. I could be really demanding and insist that we all celebrate Christmas and Easter exactly as I did as a kid, but where would that get me? I suppose it'd get me a one-way ticket to Resentmentville.

Raising a family, just like the marriage itself, is full of compromises. I care deeply that my wife's and daughters' needs are met. I make sure that I deliver a consistent message about their Jewish identity. I enjoy helping Bonnie teach them about

Judaism—both the culture and the religion. At the same time, I also feel that it is important to meet a few needs of my own. After all, it works both ways. I don't want to be the one building up resentment, year after year.

I do have my short list of things about being Christian that are important to me. Bonnie knows how sincere I am in nurturing a Jewish household, and she, in return, makes sure to take care of my needs. During Christmas, I have a tree—right there in the family room. I know some people have difficulty working such a strong symbol into their family dynamics. However, it works in our situation. Everyone in our house knows that this is Dad's tree. Bonnie and the girls help me decorate it, but they know they are Jewish and Hanukkah is their holiday. They do not celebrate both. Because of this arrangement, I feel less uptight about teaching my daughters a few things about my religion and culture. Having the Christmas tree in our home brings back a lot of happy childhood memories. Not having it would be a mistake. Being an interfaith family doesn't mean we have to sterilize the house of one of our religions. The last thing in the world I want to feel is that I can't celebrate my own holidays.

While the Christmas tree is often one of the biggest hot-button issues of interfaith families (to tree or not to tree), to us it is not the most important. First of all, it matters more to my family what we do the other 364 days of the year in teaching our daughters about being Jewish. Second, it matters more to me that I work on being a good Christian every day of the year. For instance, I enjoy accompanying Bonnie and the girls to temple. In addition, on Sundays and the Christian holidays, I like to go to my church. It's part of being Protestant. Occasionally, and especially on Christmas, I like for my wife and daughters to come with me. This is not because I want them to listen to the sermon and hopefully convert. I just like the company. There's nothing better than having your family around when something is important to you.

Fortunately for me, I have that support from my family. I know this is the biggest gift of all that they can give me. As the only non-Jew in the family, I sometimes wonder if I'll feel lonely, out of place, or even sheepish about observing my own religion. Because Bonnie and I try so hard to accommodate each other's needs when going about our daily lives, I've managed to feel fulfilled.

At 6:00 the morning after the Tooth Fairy visited, Gabbi came running into our bedroom, jumped on top of us, and yelled, "The Tooth Fairy came! The Tooth Fairy came!" As she threw her pint-sized bear hug around my neck, I was reminded once more that, yes, my most important needs were being met.

OTHER VOICES

When needs are met in a relationship, they often lessen in intensity; when needs remain unmet, they continue to carry significance (and possible resentment!). Sometimes, a partner in an interfaith relationship may experience a feeling of "aloneness" as holidays approach. The best antidote for this feeling may be talking to your partner about what you need for yourself and why you need it.

When Laurie, a Catholic, was engaged to Martin, a Conservative Jew, she was feeling sad and lonely as the December holidays approached. She told her fiancé, "This Christmas I need a really *big* Christmas tree." Fortunately, before Martin reacted, he asked her what this really big tree meant to her. Laurie's memory of the really big tree was connected to her childhood memories of happy holidays before her parents divorced. Listening to her explain her needs enabled Martin to understand the meaning of the tree for Laurie—even though he might have wanted to say, "No way." That year, Martin found Laurie the biggest blue spruce that could fit into a small apartment. She was very grateful and viewed the tree as Martin's way of acknowledging her needs.

Every year, Martin still asks Laurie if she needs her big tree, because he knows that the Christmas tree holds such significant childhood memories for the person he loves. Since Laurie knows that Martin is willing to fulfill her needs, the needs are no longer so pressing for her. Surrounded by her husband and children, she celebrates Christmas with her sister's family and her mom, helping them to decorate a very large blue spruce and meeting her need for a close and united family.

CHAPTER 20

Why I Have Chosen to Maintain My Christian Identity

What a relief. I had just finished doing a reading at Barnes and Noble Booksellers and had breezed through a relatively easy question and answer session. Everything was over and I was putting my coat on when a good friend of mine came up and asked me the most difficult question of the day: "How do you feel being the only Christian in your Jewish family?"

I told her to wait for my next reading and submit her questions in writing one week in advance to give me time to prepare. Seeing that she wasn't going to let me off the hook that easily, I had to stop and think of a way to express my feelings accurately. After all, this was a potential minefield of emotions for anyone in an interfaith family. Further, she wanted to know how I felt about my children not believing in Jesus as the Son of God.

She wasn't trying to be rude—and I certainly didn't take it that way. I'd known her for quite a while. I knew that she was a devout Christian and one who liked to take part in spirited conversations about religion. She was not a person who judged others based on their beliefs. She was just genuinely curious.

I told her that honestly sometimes it was hard on me. There

had been times when I'd wondered if I'd made the right choice. If I believed in my faith so much, how could I allow my own children not to believe in it? Would it be better if I converted to Judaism? Before the kids were born, I thought that there was a chance that I would feel like a black sheep in my own family.

However, when Bonnie and I were married, we decided to focus on the similarities of our religions. We knew that Judaism and Christianity had some fundamental differences, but there was so much more that the two had in common—especially the morals and values that they both taught. We felt that there was a way to make this work, without either one of us having to give up our faith.

In addition, we decided that we would raise our children in a way that celebrated their Judaism but also let them know that being Jewish was just a part of who they were. By helping our girls to understand it this way, we had demonstrated that sometimes family members had different faiths—just as they also had different physical and personality characteristics—and that was okay.

I told my friend that since our daughters were born, I had yet to feel like an outsider in my own home. My daughters knew full well that we had different religions. However, it really had been enjoyable for me to help them learn about Judaism. At the same time, it had been a lot of fun watching them make an effort to include me. The previous year, after we lit the first candle for Hanukkah, everyone yelled, "Happy Hanukkah!" While the hootin' and hollerin' was going on, my daughter reached over to me, pulled me down to her level, and whispered in my ear, "Merry Christmas, Dad." For a "daddy-daughter moment," you just couldn't get any better than that.

As far as my own children not believing that Jesus was the

Messiah, well, I had never been one to say which religion in this world was the correct one. While my faith has always been strong, my daughters and I still loved the same God, and that was good enough for me. The important factor here was that Bonnie and I were raising them in a faith that had wonderful traditions and taught excellent values. The last thing we wanted was for them to grow up without any religion at all.

My friend seemed satisfied with my answers, and we gathered up our kids and headed for the parking lot. She wasn't looking for a justification of why I had chosen the way I had. Rather, she was merely asking about something that was completely foreign to her. She and her husband were not only both Protestant, they were also of the same exact denomination.

I don't know if she felt that my choices were something that would have ever worked for her if she were in my shoes. I wouldn't expect them to. I have never been foolish enough to believe that everyone would agree with me on this issue. It is a tough one, and people handle it in different ways.

In fact, people often ask me why I have not converted to Judaism as one way to address the issue of our mixed-religion family. When Bonnie and I were dating and trying to figure out how we would make our interfaith marriage work, I looked at every option. It didn't take me long, however, to know that I would not convert. Conversion would have been convenient, because it would have meant that my wife, kids, and I could all practice the same religion. But convenience is not why people should convert. It has to feel truly right. I don't feel that I can leave my religion. Is letting my parents down a factor? Oh, sure. But, ultimately both my parents and I know that it would be my decision to make.

I am a Protestant. I grew up this way, and my faith is as

strong as ever. It's who I am. But it's not all I am. The Keen family mostly traces its roots back to, among other places, Clan Gunn of the Highlands of Scotland. I like to celebrate my ancestral background, even if it's more for fun than anything else. I believe that every American has a heritage and should be proud of it. That's what makes our country great. It's what unifies us—we're all from someplace else. I love teaching my girls about the places where their ancestors were born. I think it's wonderful that they learn about these people from Scotland, Ireland, Sweden, Germany, Lithuania, Russia, and Poland. What a crew. And now, I am proud to say, there are some Keens who happen to be Jewish. I love it.

Though I am firmly rooted in my Protestant background, I do not, however, feel that conversion is the wrong choice for other people. You can still be proud of your heritage and adopt a new religion and culture. I have friends who have converted to Judaism. I think that they've made the right decision for their family. They are doing very well, and I am happy for them. They contribute positively to the Jewish community and are very involved in teaching their children about Judaism. I believe that their path was no easier than mine. While it works for them, it just wouldn't be right for me.

In short, I feel that I am the luckiest guy on earth. I have kept my religion while also having had the opportunity to learn about another great religion and culture. I get to have my cake and eat it, too. I'm a Christian who is fortunate enough to help raise a Jewish family. In my eyes, it's the best of both worlds.

OTHER VOICES

Unlike a couple who shares the same religious background, an interfaith couple cannot take for granted what holidays you will celebrate as a family or how you will celebrate them. Sonya, who is Episcopalian, and Henry, who is Jewish, made the decision to raise their children as Jews. Sonya was comfortable with the decision they made for their family. Her parents had belonged to an active church community, and she knew how important religious community could be for children. She enjoyed the traditions and practices of Judaism and the way that it was structured to bring the family together. Then one day, when her oldest child was five and beginning to ask questions about God and religion, he asked why she never went to church. After all, he and his father and brother were all Jewish, and they went to synagogue. How could she really be Episcopalian if she never went to church?

After Sonya caught her breath, she realized that she had been feeling inauthentic for a long time. It wasn't that she felt she was faking being Jewish. She was very clear with her children that they were Jews and that they were a Jewish family, even though Mommy was Episcopalian. But she realized that she no longer felt authentically religious or spiritual. Here she was, teaching her children to believe in God and to go synagogue on Shabbat to pray, but she wasn't living out those same things herself.

That night, Sonya and Henry had a long and challenging conversation. Sonya voiced her need to be part of a church prayer experience and to attend church as regularly as possible. At first Henry was very uncomfortable. He was worried that Sonya regretted her decision to raise their children as Jews and might not want to be involved in the synagogue anymore.

Sonya reassured him that that wasn't the case at all, but that she needed to both fulfill her own religious needs and serve as an authentic religious role model, albeit not a Jewish one, for their children. After they talked some more, they both felt that they would be able to work out a way for Sonya to meet her own needs while still sticking to the decisions they had made about their family life.

CHAPTER 21

Seeing the World through Jewish Eyes

Helping to raise a Jewish family has exposed me to a whole new culture. You can even call it an American subculture. Learning about Judaism, its religion and way of life, has opened my mind to a lot of new perspectives. I look at current events differently. I use more Yiddish words than ever before. I now see and understand things in a new way.

I think that one of the best parts about helping to raise a Jewish family is that I understand a lot more jokes now. I've learned so much about Jewish culture that I get subtle bits of humor that I never used to. Jewish humor is actually a big part of American culture. Just look at how many Jewish comedians, writers, and actors there are: Jerry Seinfeld, Larry David, Eugene Levy, Rita Rudner, Billy Crystal, and many more. These talented artists write material that's funny to every American. But, they will often mix in a few Jewish elements that can only be understood by people familiar with Jewish culture.

I can honestly say that a lot of the humor went right over my head before I met Bonnie. Most of the time, I wasn't even aware that there was humor I was missing. Before Bonnie, one of my favorite comedians was Billy Crystal. When he was on

Saturday Night Live, he would do a skit called the "Joe Franklin Show." It was always "brought to you by matzah by Streit's. For the unleavened experience of a lifetime." I would sit there and wonder, "What on earth is he talking about?" I kind of knew what matzah was. It was those cracker thingies.

It wasn't until Bonnie invited me to a first Passover seder that I finally understood. During this holiday, Jews should not eat foods that are leavened (made with yeast). They eat special "kosher for Passover" foods. Matzah is the staple diet during this time. You eat these wafers by themselves, sometimes with butter or jam, sometimes with eggs and cottage cheese. Kosher food companies sell cakes and other treats made with matzah meal. They even make a cereal that looks (but doesn't taste) like Cheerios. Matzah is not made with yeast and, therefore, is kosher for Passover. Well, what should I see there in the kitchen during Passover? Right next to the bottle of Manischewitz kosher blackberry wine, sat—get this—a box of Streit's matzah. I just about flipped. It was an actual company. Suddenly, years of repeating that slogan, "For the unleavened experience of a lifetime," finally made sense. It *was* funny after all.

Getting to know Bonnie was the beginning of my Jewish humor education. My edification didn't come all at once, though. It took time. During our first year of dating, we rented Woody Allen's *Annie Hall.* Midway through it, I couldn't take it anymore. I didn't understand any of it. Meanwhile, Bonnie sat on the couch, just howling with laughter. She tried to explain what was so hilarious, but there was just too much Jewish shtick (look it up) for me to comprehend so quickly. Fifteen years later, I got up the courage to watch it again. This time, I finished the whole movie. It was a lot funnier than I remembered it. Woody's neuroses made a lot more sense after years of listening to the humorous stories and jokes that Bonnie's family had told me.

One of the funny things about Jewish humor is that once you understand it and people know that you'll find it funny, they tell you a lot more jokes. Bonnie's stepdad even includes me on his e-mail joke list. Here's one he sent recently (skip it if you've heard it before):

A guy named Goldstein gets marooned on a desert island. First thing he does is build a hut to live in. A few months go by, and he makes the hut a little bigger by adding on a bedroom and dining room. After a few more months, it looks like he could be there a while, so he builds himself a synagogue. A year later he decides to build a second synagogue.

Finally, after four years of living all alone on the island, a ship comes by. He signals it with a fire on the beach. The ship sees him and sends a rescue party. The crew lands on the beach, and the captain steps off.

Goldstein gives him a big hug. "Thank you for saving me."

The captain, seeing the buildings that Goldstein has erected, exclaims, "Wow! You've really been busy here. Did you build all this?"

"Yes, I did."

"What's that building there?"

"That's my house, complete with bedroom and dining room."

"What's that structure there?"

"That's my temple where I worship."

"What's that building next to it?"

"Oh, that's another synagogue."

"You worship at both this temple and the one next to it?"

"What, that temple? I wouldn't set foot in that temple!"

I told this joke to some non-Jewish friends and family. Guess what. It bombed. What I'm finding even funnier than the joke itself are the various reactions to the subtlety of the humor. Don't feel bad if you don't get it either. In time, you might. It's not a reflection of intelligence; it's a reflection of familiarity with a culture, a people's ability to make fun of itself.

In addition, the more time you spend around a certain group, the more you start using the group's language. Think about high school. You and your friends had a few phrases and words that anyone outside of your peer group would have had a difficult time understanding. And, by the time the old folks caught on to your lingo, you'd moved on to new words. I've been out of high school long enough to look foolish saying, "That's so lit!" or, "On fleek." In fact, by the time I learned what these meant, the kids had already moved on to something else they wouldn't tell me. I think I'll just stick to "Cool."

Medical professionals also have their own linguistic references. Doctors and nurses are always talking about EKGs and taking "meds" and giving shots "sub Q." After being around the doctor's office long enough, you start to understand what they mean. You even start talking like them. "Honey, I'm running down to the pharmacy to pick up my 'script.'" But, admit it. When you first heard these words and expressions, you were clueless as to what they meant.

That's exactly how I was in the Jewish world. Only now, I was learning words and phrases of real languages—Hebrew and Yiddish. It was bad enough that Bonnie was a law student while we were engaged. I had quite a time when we were around her classmates, trying to keep up with all the talk about "Con law," "torts," and "civ pro." Now, on every visit to her parents' home, it seemed that I learned a new word or expression.

I was also surprised to find that I had been using some Yiddish and Hebrew words for years before I met Bonnie—words like *shmuck*. This by, the way, is not as nice a word as I had thought. I found out that a common phrase, "the whole megillah," which I had used plenty of times in the past, actually comes from the word for "scroll" and refers to the reading of the whole story of the holiday of Purim, from the Scroll of Esther.

It wasn't long until I started using more Yiddish and Hebrew in my everyday speech. After a workout at the gym, I'd say, "That was a good *shvitz* [sweat]." After my daughters were born, I started saying things like, "Don't bump your *keppe* [head]." Or, pinching their chubby cheeks, I'd comment, "What a *punim* [face]." Even right now, I'm getting a little *verklempt* (choked up) thinking about how fast those kids are growing up. When you hear it enough around you, you get comfortable with it and start using it yourself.

Sometimes I feel a certain sense of "being in the know" using these phrases. When we go to Michigan football games, we usually sit in the same section, with the same people who've sat there for years around us. At one game last year, a guy and his son, who sit down the row from us, had to leave at halftime. When asked by the group why they were leaving early, the father replied that they were going to the son's bar mitzvah (why they were at the game at all that day, I'll never know—true-blue fans, I guess).

"Congratulations!" everyone told them as they sidestepped their way down the row to the aisle. "*Mazal tov!*" I automatically said when they finally got to me. The smile and thanks they gave me were not really any different than those that they gave to everyone else. However, the subtlety of my choice of words brought a hint of a knowing look in their eyes.

Using the Hebrew phrase for "congratulations" gave me a certain sense of belonging to another group. Although I am not Jewish, I can now identify with the culture. Yes, the humor makes more sense now, but so do more serious things related to Judaism, like the Holocaust. When I'm listening to the news, any mention of current events in Israel causes my ears to perk up. It's all so much more relevant to me now, because it is relevant to *my* family.

I am not Jewish, but my nuclear family is. I'm proud of my wife and daughters. They include me in their culture and religion—and I *feel* included. After all, I have helped teach it to Gabbi and Molly. That is very important to me. Not having that sense of inclusion was a big fear of mine before Bonnie and I married. Today, not only am I a part of my wife and daughters' group, but I also have the ability to think and feel it. I still enjoy belonging to my Scottish-American, Protestant group, but it's a warm feeling being able to see the world through Jewish eyes, as well.

CHAPTER 22

Do You Feel Connected to Your Family?

Deciding in which religion to raise our kids was our most difficult decision. I was nervous that I wouldn't feel connected to them if they were raised Jewish. I had no idea if they would relate to me or see me as part of the family if I were of a different religion. I wasn't sure that I'd know how to raise them in another faith. To tell the truth though, I think that I would have been uncertain of what to do even if I'd married a Christian. There is no operating manual that doctors give you when your child is born. Yet now that I'm actually a dad, I realize that most of my fears were off base.

Don't take that the wrong way. I'm not belittling the feelings of anyone who might be in that situation. Those are very real anxieties that should legitimately be addressed. However, after all these years helping Bonnie raise our children (and they are preparing to leave the nest), I see that I connect with them in so many other ways that I can't help but feel that I'm an integral part of their lives.

I was the one who coached their soccer teams—a cute bunch of ball-kickin', dandelion-pickin' girls, called the Ladybugs. I took Molly to gymnastics every Saturday morning, where I watched her bounce and tumble her way around the gym. The girls and I still go to the museum together, where we stare in awe at the dinosaurs. We visit the planetarium to see a show about the stars in the sky. We collect interesting rocks and try to identify them. We dig up brachiopod fossils near our house and take them to that same museum to have them identified. (Incidentally, we were very pleased to learn that a brachiopod was a mollusk-type creature that lived about 450 million years ago, when Michigan was covered by a sea.) Each one of these activities is something that my daughters associate with me. They are fun things that we do together and continue to talk about at the dinner table.

However, connecting to my children isn't just about taking them places. I'm the guy they expected to sing them a song at night, while I gently tickled their arms in a vain attempt to get them to fall asleep. Though Bonnie and I both read stories to the girls, I'm the guy they expected to change the words around and make up new stories. Their mom may be the one who was best at kissing their boo-boos when they got hurt, but I was the one who was roughhousing with them in the family room and caused the injury. Funny thing is, they always came back for more. As young adults, we still share connections. For instance, Gabbi and I share a love of *Star Wars*. Molly and I love to rent comedies.

I am not at all an outsider in my family. I don't know why I couldn't see it before we got married. But until you've actually experienced life as a parent, you have no way of knowing how well you'll connect with your children or in what ways.

What's become even more surprising for me, however, is the way that I'm also able to relate to my wife and children on a Jewish level. In the first year of our marriage, Bonnie and I took an "Introduction to Judaism" class. I wanted to learn more about what I had gotten myself into. She went along for a "refresher course" and to support me. We had always said that raising our family would be a joint effort, so taking the class together felt like the right thing to do.

Taking this class was one of the best things I have done. Learning about Judaism has helped me to become more comfortable with Bonnie's religion, culture, and family traditions. It has also given me a strong knowledge base from which I've been able to help teach my daughters about their faith. So far, I haven't gotten a comment like "What do you know about Moses, Dad? You're not Jewish." Gabbi and Molly now associate me with so much of their religious education that I don't think I ever will hear anything like that.

Joining the Reform synagogue here in town has also been beneficial to our family. Do I feel like an outsider in the synagogue? No way. I may have been the guy who drove the kids to the museum, but I was also the one who took them to religious school on Saturdays. Our rabbi, Robert Levy (who has since retired), was more than welcoming to our interfaith family. He encouraged me to participate in the services in any way that I felt comfortable. During one of my first children's services, he even made sure that I got a chance to see the Torah up close. In the past, I had only viewed it from afar. Unexpectedly, it was a very heartfelt moment for me. It was pure acceptance of who I was. I was welcomed for just being me.

Where some congregations may be losing members, our synagogue is overflowing. Rabbi Levy's philosophy was to be as inclusive as possible. "Often, there is a mind-set in the Jewish world that it's all about numbers," he says. "How many people can we count as Jews? Instead, we should be focusing on the people as human beings and reaching out to them. When you lower the barriers to entry, everybody wins." The whole synagogue staff shares this philosophy, from the cantor to the director of religious education—both wonderful people who expect me to be as involved with my daughters' experience as much as any other parent.

In addition, knowing that there are other families in our situation in the congregation has enhanced my sense of belonging. When we go to temple, I'm surrounded by friends who are in the same interfaith situation that we are. It's comforting to know that you're not the only one out there who's trying to make a go of this. We have many friends who provide a great support group for us. It's been more than helpful to have bounced ideas off of each other and have shared hilarious stories about how our kids perceived their mixed-faith world.

Our friends Teresa and Barry, one such interfaith couple, told us how they like to go to a certain place for brunch on Sundays. It's normally very crowded, but if you get there early enough, you can beat the rush of people who show up after they get out of church. One Sunday, while racing to get there early, their then five-year-old, Claire, shouted out from the back of the minivan, "Hurry up before the Christians get there!"

The fact that we get together with many of these intermarried families socially outside the temple makes it all the more enjoyable when we see them at temple functions. We try to attend as many of the family activities there as possible. They're a lot of fun, and our kids get to see *both* of their parents, as well as friends, participating in their religious activities.

Through the temple, I had gotten to know Rabbi Levy more and more. He was always glad to see us there. Just as important, he was always welcoming to me, the Christian parent—not the outsider. Today his successor, Rabbi Josh Whinston, shares the same mind-set and extends the same warm welcome to our family. Because of this open attitude, I have always known that I belong and have a role.

I've learned that you can feel as included or excluded as you want. It depends on the amount of effort you put into being there for your family and wanting to feel connected. It has been important for me to make the effort to connect and be involved, and it has paid off. It hasn't been without complications, but we have been able to create a cohesive interfaith family. Over the years, I've found that my daughters don't need to put forth a conscious effort to include me or acknowledge the religious differences between them and myself.

During the Christmas seasons when the girls were young, I would wake up every day to a fresh pile of Christmas cards that Gabbi and Molly had drawn for me with construction paper and crayons. They knew from an early age that my religion was different from theirs. But I am their dad and an integral part of their lives. I am important for the fatherly love that I have always given them by playing dress-up in the family room, discovering how bubbles work at the science museum, or taking them on college visits. I am also important to their religious identity. This was clear to me very early in their lives when I would arrive home from work on Friday evenings and was greeted at the door by two little girls who were as excited as birds around a feeder. "Daddy's home!" they would shout. "Now we can have Shabbat!" Today, I am usually waiting for them to get home from their various activities before we can start Shabbat. And as they begin to travel around the world exploring life without me, I know that I will always share that special bond a dad has with his daughters. Do I feel connected? How could I not?

CONCLUSION

If you've ever wondered whether you were doing the right thing, you often didn't fully discover the answer until you dove right in. Before Bonnie and I were married, I wondered, "Will I regret my decision? What if it doesn't work? Will I be isolated?" These were all questions that I asked myself over and over. I think most brides and grooms have these feelings, even without the intermarriage issue.

Despite the uncertainty, there was this little voice inside reminding me that I loved Bonnie. Would God really want me to lose my chance at spending the rest of my life with this wonderful person, just because our backgrounds were different? No. I decided that diving in was the only course of action.

I have no regrets. Our marriage and family dynamics haven't been perfect. Nothing in life is. However, our love is strong, and so is our desire to work things out. Even after our wedding day, I'd occasionally wonder how our children would turn out or if we should change how we approach certain holidays. However, we are committed to being flexible and to keep trying. I don't think that there's any issue we can't conquer.

Although there is a high rate of divorce in interfaith marriages, I believe that different-religion couples often have an advantage over same-religion couples. They're so used to communicating and solving their religious issues that they're ready when other problems inevitably hit the relationship. They've already established their model for working things out. This is, of course, easier when done before the wedding. However, it's never too late to start. Hopefully more interfaith couples will realize this advantage and discover that their differences, though complicated, can truly be a gift.

A reporter once asked me what I thought was the most unfortunate aspect of interfaith relationships. I replied that it is sad to see two people end their relationship with each other because they can't get past their differences in religion. I had just written an article for *InterfaithFamily* about how my family handles the December dilemma. A couple of days after its publication, I received an e-mail from a woman who had read my article. The day before, she had broken up with her boyfriend, because they didn't think that they could possibly resolve their interfaith issues. They had been dating for a number of years and were trying to figure out how they could live with each other and raise children. She was Christian, and he was Jewish.

After reading through several articles on *InterfaithFamily*, she realized that she and her boyfriend had made a mistake. She didn't yet know what the right answer was for her particular situation, but she was now inspired to find out. If other people could be successful at intermarriage, so could they. She told me that she was going to call her boyfriend and give it another try.

I think she was glad just to know that there are many other people out there in the same quandary. Few people go looking for someone of the other faith to marry. Many people even oppose interfaith relationships altogether. That's fine. However, whether you're all for intermarrying or dead set against it, you can't escape the fact that people voluntarily and involuntarily fall into these relationships. Fortunately, there are ways to help them create a path to having a happy and feasible future together.

The experiences that I've related in this book are just one family's way of trying to make sense of this mixed-up world in which we live. I have many friends in successful interfaith relationships who have come up with different solutions. My hope in writing this book has been to share what has worked for us. If you learn nothing else from this book, please understand that there is a workable solution to just about any interfaith relationship. If two people love each other and they have the desire to find the right formula and be honest with each other about their individual expectations and needs, they can succeed. Like a Yom Kippur congregation in a break-fast buffet line, there shouldn't be any stopping them.

EPILOGUE

Trading Places:
When Children Start Dating

I had just finished giving a talk at the Union for Reform Judaism (URJ) Biennial Conference, and it was time for the question and answer session. As I scanned the room for raised hands, I spotted a woman in the third row. She looked harmless enough, so I called on her. "What would you do if your own daughter started dating someone who wasn't Jewish?" she asked with an apologetic look on her face.

BAM! This was no softball question. In fact, it startled me. Stalling for an answer, I said, "I would disown her."

Fortunately, people knew that I was kidding. And while they laughed, it gave me time to think of what to say, in my own honest feelings. I told her that I would, of course, be supportive. I mean, I couldn't be hypocritical of everything Bonnie and I had striven so hard to make work. I would have to tell my daughters, when they start dating, that their mother and I are here for them. We can offer advice based on our experience but would not force the decisions we made in our relationship on them.

A few years later, when Gabbi and Molly actually started dabbling in dating, I suddenly realized that I got it. I totally got it! Now I knew a little how my own father-in-law must have felt when Bonnie and I began dating. Sure, sure, my daughters weren't seriously dating, but it got me looking down the road to when they would be. I felt that after all the time, energy, and love that had gone into raising them as Jews, I could see myself hoping that they would never give up that part of themselves.

When they start dating seriously, I want them to find someone who will make them happy and treat them well. However, I now have a newfound understanding and respect for all of the parents out there who have to deal with people like me—coming in with my different religion, taking their daughters away, and raising new families under a different roof. Fortunately, I also can now see how well things are working for our nuclear and extended families, and it calms me right down.

So, I will continue to plan on letting Gabbi and Molly know that their mother and I are there for them if they ever need help in figuring out the complexities of interfaith relationships. And if they don't want to talk, at least I can recommend a good book.

INSIDE INTERMARRIAGE
DISCUSSION GUIDE

This discussion guide was written by Dr. Paula Brody, who has worked with hundreds of interfaith families over a twenty-five-year career as director of outreach programs and training for the Union for Reform Judaism in Boston. Dr. Brody has led national training programs for clergy, educators, counselors, and Jewish professionals to understand the complex issues involved in interfaith family relationships. She developed the "Yours, Mine and Ours" group model for enabling interfaith couples to strengthen their communication skills in a supportive small group setting with other couples.

This book and the following discussion questions focus on the need to resolve issues and keep communication open in an interfaith family. Indeed, communication is the key to working through issues in *any* long-term relationship, and it is particularly true in interfaith ones.

Inside Intermarriage is essential reading for interfaith couples, whether they are dating, engaged, married, or married with children. Clergy, educators, marriage counselors, family therapists, and many others of all faith backgrounds will benefit from reading this book and taking an in-depth look at some of the challenging issues that interfaith couples may face.

How to Use This Guide

Couples

This guide was written primarily for you. Use the chapter-specific questions to help you and your partner begin a dialogue about these issues. You can also use them to jump-start conversation with family, if needed.

Professionals

Facilitated discussion—whether in individual counseling or in a series of group sessions—can be valuable to couples. If the discussion is part of a series in congregations or other settings, couples will find it meaningful to read several chapters of *Inside Intermarriage* before coming together to share responses to the questions. These conversations are optimally led by a social worker or another professional or lay leader trained in encouraging group discussions. (Interfaith couples may be reluctant to discuss their needs and issues openly if the group is led by clergy.)

Certain questions may be better for a full-group discussion, and other questions might be best discussed in a smaller group, with an opportunity to reconvene to share insights.

It is also recommended to address some questions with the Jewish partners in one group and those from other faith backgrounds in another group. This discussion format often leads to lively and very honest dialogue, especially when the questions focus on issues around holidays or parents. A skilled facilitator can help the partners understand the point of view of those in the other group. Strong bonds of friendship among the couples may develop from these multiple group discussion sessions.

Note: Because *Inside Intermarriage* presents the point of view of a parent who has made a clear decision to raise children within Judaism, group sessions focusing on the book may not be appropriate for a group of interfaith couples who have not yet made any decisions about the religious identity of their children. Using the book in this setting would likely be seen as presenting a biased view of the future choices that these couples might make or interpreted as pressure to make Jewish choices.

Families and In-Laws

Inside Intermarriage is also a helpful resource for groups of parents (current or future grandparents) whose adult children are in interfaith relationships. As with discussion sessions for couples themselves, families might read several chapters in advance and discuss them in a facilitated group setting. Parents can use the discussion questions "to step into the shoes" of the partner from another faith. The book and the discussion questions can help future in-laws be more sensitive to their son- or daughter-in-law who has decided to raise children in the partner's faith, which can strengthen future family relationships.

The following questions are for parents and families:

- As parents of adult children in an interfaith relationship, what can you do to make someone feel more comfortable in your home, especially someone who loves and is loved by your son or daughter?
- How can you show love to your son or daughter by your sensitivity to the needs of his or her partner?
- If you show acceptance of your son's or daughter's choice of a life partner, does this mean that you are neglecting your own values or possibly acknowledging your approval of intermarriage? How is acceptance different from approval?
- What are some ways you will show your unconditional love to your grandchildren?
- Keeping in mind that sharing family holidays and life-cycle celebrations will be cherished milestone moments for your children and grandchildren, what are the active steps you can take to enhance these moments in a loving way?
- Think about your own grandparents or other older adults in your life as you were growing up. What were the shared moments that you cherish the most? What are the moments you will want your grandchildren to look back upon and cherish?
- How can you help support your son's or daughter's decision?
- How can you help your son- or daughter-in-law learn about your religion? And how can you learn about his or her religion as well?
- How can you identify and handle your own complicated emotions about your son's or daughter's religious journey if it doesn't follow the path you expected?

Chapter 1. When We First Discover Our Religious and Cultural Differences

- How did you first realize that your partner was raised in a different faith tradition?
- What assumptions did you have about individuals or families of that religion?
- How have you overcome these assumptions and better understand that faith tradition?
- What active steps can you take or have you taken to learn more about each other's faith backgrounds?

Chapter 2. The Relationship Turns Serious: Now What?

- Share with your partner several experiences when you felt you were a minority in a majority culture or setting. How did these experiences make you feel?
- What would you describe as the differences between religion and culture?
- What do you see as a few differences in culture between Christians and Jews?
- Although you may have many conversations about your religious and cultural differences, what are the most important things you share in common with your partner? With your partner's family?

Chapter 3. When Did I Become a "Non-Jew"?

- Think about when you have felt excluded for being the "other." Whether this was a gender, age, cultural, or religious difference, how did this make you feel?
- Think about a time when you experienced something new and different. How did that first experience make you feel? How did those feelings change as you became more familiar and comfortable with this experience?
- How can you help your partner feel more comfortable and avoid some awkward moments at family, community, or religious events?

- How can you ensure that important aspects of your partner's faith are realized in his or her life and in your life together?
- Share with your partner three aspects of your faith background that you most value and why. In your relationship, how can you include some of these most valued aspects of each other's faith background in your life together?

Chapter 4. What Religion Would Our Children Be?

- What are the three most important things each of you would need if you choose to raise children in your partner's faith? Why are these things important to you?
- As a loving partner, could you meet your partner's needs as expressed above? What can you actively do to meet your partner's needs? Express this to your partner.
- If your children are being raised in your religious tradition, what can you do to ensure that your partner is a part of the special religious rituals you share with your children? How can you include your partner's family? What can you do to make every effort to meet the needs of your partner?

Chapter 5. Telling My Parents We're Raising Jewish Kids

- Share with your partner what aspects of your faith, as transmitted by your family, you value most.
- Talk about why these traditions, family rituals, or values matter in your lives. How can you incorporate some of these into your life together?
- Your parents want to feel that you value the way they raised you. How can you enable them to feel that you do value your family rituals and traditions?
- What steps can you take to make both sets of parents feel included in the rituals and traditions you have chosen for your family?

Chapter 6. When Nothing Else Will Do, Have a "Jewish-ish" Wedding

- List the things about your wedding ceremony and reception that are important to each of you. Circle the top three things on each of your lists, and discuss why they are important to you. What compromises can you make to incorporate at least one or perhaps all three into your wedding day?
- Make a separate list of the things about your wedding and reception that may be important to each set of your parents. Realizing that your marriage may be something your parents have been envisioning for many years, what compromises might you make to meet at least one or two of your parents' needs on your wedding day?
- "To see your face is like seeing the face of God" (Genesis 33:10). How does your feeling of connection to the sacred express itself in your love for each other? How might you wish to reflect the sacredness of your love for each other in your wedding ceremony?

Chapter 7. How This Christian Came to Give His Daughters Hebrew Names

- What important steps will you each take to ensure that both partners feel involved in the transmission of religious identity to your children? What important roles can each of you play during the special religious moments in your child's life? How can you help your partner feel comfortable and a part, not apart, of these special moments in your family life?
- What can both of you do to help all your parents feel comfortable and a part, not apart, of special religious rituals and traditions in your family life? What can you do to especially engage and include the parents whose faith identity may be different from their grandchildren to ensure that they feel included in your family's life-cycle ceremonies and holiday celebrations?

Chapter 8. Bat Mitzvah: The Natural Next Step

• Some partners in interfaith relationships worry that they will not be a full part of their child's life if their children are not raised in their religion. What are some ways you can you feel a connection to your children and support your children at life-cycle moments, apart from religion?

• How do you see your role in supporting and nurturing your children's religious identity?

• What questions or concerns might be on the mind of family members from other faith backgrounds as they anticipate this momentous life-cycle event? How might you respond to their concerns or answer their questions?

Chapter 9. Losing a Loved One

• Different faith traditions have very different rituals around loss and mourning. Talk about these differences and how you might engage in various traditions at a time of significant loss. How can you support your partner at a time of his or her grieving?

• Tell your partner what you remember and how you felt about deaths in your circle of family/friends/community that occurred in your childhood and young adult lives.

• What do you recall about the religious traditions (or lack thereof) that surrounded these times of loss and mourning? Share these memories with your partner. How do you understand the religious rituals and traditions that surrounded those moments?

• Burial can be a challenging issue for interfaith families. Explore the burial laws of cemeteries when you envision internment for members of your family. Can you be buried together in these cemeteries? What plan for a family burial might you choose?

Chapter 10. Questions about God from the Backseat

- Teaching children about God is challenging for most parents, and this is especially true for partners in an interfaith relationship. Sometimes, it is optimal to answer your children's questions with another question, such as "What do you believe about God?" Chances are you, as parents, will never be fully prepared for many of the questions your children ask, but you can prepare a bit by beginning these conversations now with your partner.

- Share with your partner what you believed about God when you were a child and how these beliefs have evolved. What does God mean in your life now? At what moments do you feel the presence of God?

- What do you want your children to believe about God?

- How might you and your partner be clear and consistent in ways that reinforce the religious identity decisions you have made for your children?

Chapter 11. "Don't They Know I'm Jewish?" Our Children Start to Comprehend Their Jewish Identity

- Think of a time when you felt quite anxious about unknown aspects of your future. What helped you move through these feelings of anxiety?

- What are some of the important things about your hobbies, interests, and life passions that you will want to share with your children? How do you envision teaching them about these interests? Share with your partner how you developed these interests and who may have mentored you. How do you envision being a mentor to your children?

- As your children learn new things that are not familiar to you— such as sports, the arts, math, or religion—how do you envision reinforcing such learning? How do you see yourselves as a parental team reinforcing this learning?

Chapter 12. Fun and Games at the Jewish Community Center

- What choices can you make together that will enable you both to feel a sense of community?
- What active steps can each of you take to feel more involved and engaged in your shared communities?
- Do you want experiences shared with your children to create opportunities to meet like-minded families? In what settings/communities do you envision making these friends?

Chapter 13. Teaching My Parents about Judaism

- Think about special shared moments you may have experienced with your own grandparents or other older adults in your life. How did these shared experiences shape you? Share with your partner memories of your grandparents or other adults who were an important influence in your life.
- What special talents or interests, beyond religion, do your parents or grandparents have that they might transmit to your children?
- How can you help your parents to feel involved in shared holidays when they are not familiar with the religious tradition? What active steps can you take to help both sets of parents become involved in your children's lives and share special milestone moments?

Chapter 14. Shabbat: The Holiday That Comes Every Week

- Shabbat offers a weekly opportunity to build family memories, whereas other holidays occur only once a year. How might you envision creating Shabbat memories in your family life? What personal touch might you bring to make these rituals special or unique for your family?
- What other special family rituals and memories might you wish to create for your children?
- What can you both do as parents to reinforce a consistent and secure sense of religious identity for your children?

Chapter 15. The High Holidays: A Time for Both of Us to Learn

- How do you want your partner to honor your religious holidays or traditions?

- Remembering that first-time experiences always feel somewhat awkward, what can you do to be an ambassador for your partner when he or she first experiences family or church/synagogue holiday rituals? What can you do to support each other so that rituals different from your traditions begin to feel more comfortable for both of you?

- How do you want your partner's extended family to acknowledge and respect your important holiday traditions? What can you do to help your partner and in-laws honor your holiday traditions? What can you do to honor their holidays and traditions that are most meaningful to them?

- How will you support each other and each other's faith during important times? How will you teach your children to respect the faith traditions of both of their parents? How will you encourage your children to respect faith traditions in their extended family?

Chapter 16. Sukkot? Never Heard of It

- Share with your partner any "magical" memories that you associate with holidays from your childhood. What makes these moments special?

- What can you do to make such experiences memorable for yourselves and your children? Are there ways to mark home holidays in a more inclusive, communal way to family or friends of other faiths?

Chapter 17. Will Santa Bring Me Presents Even If I'm Jewish?

- Share your childhood memories of the December holiday season with each other. How did those holidays make you feel, and what engendered those feelings?

- How can you acknowledge and support your partner's needs during this season?
- How can a Jewish partner honor in-laws and extended family during the Christmas season?
- Discuss with your partner why many Jewish families feel ambivalence during the Christmas season.
- How will you reinforce your children's religious identity during the December holidays? What do you see as the best ways to give clear and consistent messages to your children?
- What will you say to both sets of grandparents about how you plan to celebrate holiday celebrations throughout the year? How will you help your parents and other family reinforce the religious identity you have chosen for your children?

Chapter 18. Eggs and Plagues: Easter/Passover Issues

- Share your childhood memories of Easter or Passover. What was most special about these holidays for you, and why?
- How could you support your partner as he or she experiences Passover or Easter for the first time? What can you do to enable your partner to feel included in your unique family rituals and traditions as the years go by?

Chapter 19. If I Can't Play Santa Claus, at Least I Can Be the Tooth Fairy

- Raising children in a faith other than your own is a complex decision. If you are the recipient of such a loving gift, how can you express your appreciation of this decision to your partner?
- Share your religious needs with your partner, and discuss how far out of your comfort zone you would be willing to go to meet these needs.

Chapter 20. Why I Have Chosen to Maintain My Christian Identity
- What do you need from your partner to maintain your own faith or support your decision about conversion?
- If you have been discussing conversion to your partner's faith, what have you come to love and find truly meaningful about this new faith tradition?
- Discuss whether this decision is coming from a feeling of love for your partner and his or her faith or from feeling of pressure.
- How can you best communicate those decisions with your parents and your partner's parents?

Chapter 21. Seeing the World through Jewish Eyes
- In what ways have you come to identify as a part of your partner's cultural or religious traditions?
- How has being part of an interfaith relationship enhanced your ability to see the world through different eyes?

Chapter 22. Do You Feel Connected to Your Family?
- What are the other connections, besides religion, that each of you, as parents, might have with your children? What talents, special interests, or values, apart from religion, do you hope to transmit or share with your children?
- What moments and milestones, other than religious ceremonies, do you look forward to sharing with your children?

Conclusion
- How has communication regarding your religious differences strengthened your relationship?
- How have the decisions or compromises you have made enabled you to have the communication tools to make future choices you will inevitably face?
- How has listening to, understanding, and meeting your partner's needs enabled you both to better express your love for one another?

GLOSSARY

Note: I recognize that there are almost as many pronunciations and spellings of the following words as there are Jews. I have put them down here as my wife, my in-laws, and my Jewish extended family have taught me (unwittingly or not).

afikoman (ah-fee-KO-man) A piece of matzah that is hidden during the Passover seder, often for ransom by the parents or children, depending on individual family traditions.

baruch (bah-RUKH) The first word in many Jewish prayers. It means "blessed."

bat mitzvah / bar mitzvah (BAHT MITS-vah / BAR MITS-vah) The ceremony where a Jewish child comes of age, usually at age thirteen. Translated literally, it means "daughter/son of the commandment," or to put it another way, the age at which one is expected to take personal responsibility for the commandments. To be technically correct, one would not say, "I'm having a bat mitzvah," but, "I'm becoming a bat mitzvah."

bimah (BEE-mah) A raised platform in the synagogue from which the Torah is read and services led.

bris (BRISS) Yiddish for the circumcision ceremony. In Hebrew, *brit milah.*

b'rit bat (BRIT BAHT) The ceremony to welcome the birth of a girl. Also called by its English term, "baby naming."

b'rit milah (BRIT mee-LAH) The circumcision ceremony (removal of the foreskin of the penis). In Yiddish, "bris."

bubba or *bubbe* (BUH-buh or BUH-bee) Yiddish word for "grandmother." *Bubbe* is actually the more common of the two.

challah (KHAH-lah) The bread eaten at almost every Jewish ceremony or holiday. Sometimes its shape is braided; sometimes its shape is swirled. Though some use the expression "challah bread," it is actually redundant.

chuppah (KHUH-pah) The canopy under which the bride and groom stand in a Jewish wedding, meant to represent the home they are creating together.

dreidel (DRAY-duhl) The four-sided top spun during Hanukkah. A game is played with dreidels for *gelt* or other candy. Each side of the top has a Hebrew letter for which players give or receive candy: *nun* = you get no candy from the pot; *hay* = you get half of the pot; *shin* = you cough up candy for the pot; *gimmel* (everyone's favorite) = you win the whole pot.

El Malei Rachamim (EL mah-LAY rah-khah-MEEM) The prayer said at Jewish funerals, either at the end of the service in the synagogue, or at the gravesite. It asks God to take the soul of the deceased. Literally it means "God, full of compassion."

etrog (EHT-rogue) The fruit used during the celebration of Sukkot. It resembles a big lemon and is always paired with the *lulav*. The English word for this fruit is "citron." Ironically, about the only other time one sees this fruit is at Christmas, when it is used in breads and fruitcakes.

freilach (FRAY-lakh) Yiddish word for "happy." This term most often refers to a traditional dance of Eastern European origin. Like the hora, it is very popular at weddings.

gefilte fish (guh-FILL-teh FISH) Yiddish term for traditional Jewish food of ground-up fish balls. The fish used is usually carp, whitefish, pike, or a combination of them.

gelt (GELT) Yiddish for "money." Also refers to the chocolate coins wrapped in gold foil that are a Hanukkah mainstay. Gelt is often used for prizes when playing dreidel.

goy (GOY); pl., *goyim* (GOY-eem) Someone who is not a Jew. Sometimes its usage is considered derogatory. The literal meaning of the word is "nation" or "people."

haggadah (hah-GAH-dah) The book of prayers and songs that tells the story of Passover. Typically, everyone at the Passover seder has a copy of the haggadah and follows along with the service.

Hamotzi (hah-MOE-tsee) The blessing over the bread. Almost always, the bread is challah.

Hanukkah (HAN-u-kah) The holiday celebrating the victory of the Maccabees over the Syrians. It is often called the Festival of Lights, referring to the lighting of the eight candles of the menorah. This symbolizes the miracle of the oil that burned for eight days in the Second

Temple in Jerusalem after the Syrians were overthrown. It is actually a relatively minor Jewish holiday and is not the "Jewish Christmas," as many non-Jews believe. Literally, *Hanukkah* means "dedication."

hespeid (HES-payd) The tribute to the deceased at a funeral, much like a Christian eulogy. It is designed to summarize the accomplishments of the deceased and give comfort to the grieving.

hora (HORA) The traditional Jewish dance often seen at weddings and bar and bat mitzvah celebrations. "Hava Nagilah" is often the song played for this dance.

Kaddish (KAH-dish) Literally means "sanctification." Although there are many forms of this prayer, it is mostly known as the mourner's prayer. The majority of the words are in Aramaic, not Hebrew. It is recited not only at funerals, but also during daily services and on Shabbat.

keppe (KEH-pea) Yiddish for "head."

Kiddush (KID-ish) The blessing over the wine. It means "sanctification."

k'ri'ah (keh-REE-ah) The act of cutting one's clothing, either actually or symbolically, to represent the tearing apart that the death has caused in a mourner's life.

kugel (COO-gull) Yiddish term for a pudding or baked casserole type of dish. One common type of kugel is made with noodles and eggs. Another favorite is a potato kugel.

latkes (LOT-kahs) The potato pancakes eaten during Hanukkah. They are fried in oil, symbolic of the oil burned for eight days in the story of Hanukkah.

lulav (LOO-lav) Sprigs of palm, myrtle, and willow tied together to form one branch. It is used in ceremony, in conjunction with the *etrog*, during the holiday of Sukkot.

matzah (MAH-tsah) The unleavened bread eaten during Passover. It can come in the form of a cracker, a ball, and even a breakfast cereal. Caution: eating a lot of matzah may give one lead-belly.

matzah brei (MAH-tsah BRYE) Yiddish for a popular dish traditionally served for breakfast during Passover. It is made by dipping matzah in water and eggs, then frying them. It can be served with cottage cheese, syrup, powdered sugar, or other toppings.

mazal tov (MAH-zal TOV) Hebrew for "good luck." It is a congratulatory expression said at weddings, bar and bat mitzvah celebrations, births, or other milestones.

megillah (meh-GIL-ah) Hebrew for "scroll." Used in Yiddish to mean "the whole ball of wax." One of the most well-known of the biblical scrolls is the Book of Esther, read on the holiday of Purim. This particular story is chanted out loud on Purim, giving birth to the expression "the whole megillah."

menorah (meh-NOE-rah) A candelabrum that holds seven candles. The nine-candled version, associated with Hanukkah, is technically called a *hanukkiyah*. It has eight candles to represent the eight nights of the holiday, plus a "helper" candle, called the *shamash*, used to light the others. Today, menorahs come in all shapes and sizes, including ones that have Mickey Mouse and other Disney characters as candleholders.

milchig (MILL-khick) In kosher terms, the dairy foods (e.g., milk, cheese). When keeping kosher, it is prohibited to include meat products in a *milchig* meal.

mishpachah (mish-PUH-khah) This is the Yiddish pronunciation of the Hebrew word of the same spelling. It literally means "family." The "whole *mishpachah*" refers to everyone in the family, including extended family, relatives, and sometimes close friends.

mitzvah (MITS-vah); pl., *mitzvot* (MITS-voht) Technically a commandment, but many people think of it as a good deed.

mohel (MOY-el) A Hebrew word (MOE-hel; feminine, *mohelet*), but often pronounced in this Yiddish version. It refers to the trained professional who performs the ritual circumcision at a bris.

punim (PUH-nim) Yiddish for "face." Often said as part of the expression *shayna punim*, or "pretty face." Children duck for cover when hearing this phrase for fear of pinched cheeks.

seder (SAY-der) The ceremonial dinner of Passover, during which Jews read from the haggadah, learn about the holiday, and eat great food.

Shabbat (shah-BAHT) The Jewish Sabbath. It begins on Friday at sundown and ends Saturday at sundown. It is traditionally a time when no work should be done.

Shabbes (SHA-bis) Yiddish for "Shabbat," the Jewish Sabbath.

Shabbes goy (SHA-bis GOY) The Yiddish term for a non-Jew who has been hired (often by a synagogue) to perform various jobs that are forbidden on Shabbat.

shiksa (SHICK-sah) A derogatory Yiddish term for a non-Jewish woman or girl.

shiva (SHIH-vah) The seven-day period of mourning immediately following burial. During this time, the grieving family members primarily stay in the home and receive those paying a condolence call. It is also called "sitting shiva."

sh'loshim (sheh-loe-SHEEM) The thirty-day period of mourning. The first seven days are called "shiva." Between shiva and the end of the thirty days, the mourner is expected to resume normal activities, except for celebrations, sporting events, and other entertainment.

shmuck (SHMUCK) Despite many gentiles' cavalier use of this word, it is actually a vulgar Yiddish term for "penis."

shmutz (SHMUTZ) A Yiddish word for dirt, grime, or filth.

shofar (SHOW-far) A trumpet made from a ram's horn. It is blown at services on the holidays of Rosh Hashanah and Yom Kippur.

shtick (SHTICK) This Yiddish term is most commonly used for an actor's comedic routine. However, it can simply refer to anyone's clichéd mannerisms.

shul (shool) Yiddish word for synagogue, sometimes spelled *schul.*

shvitz (SHVITS) In Yiddish, when used as a verb, it means "to sweat"; as a noun, it means "steam bath." In Hebrew, it means to "boast or brag."

simchah (SIM-khah) A happy occasion. This is the Yiddish pronunciation. (In Hebrew, sim-KHA.)

sukkah (SOO-kah) The hut built for the fall festival of Sukkot. During this time, families often eat and even sleep in the sukkah. It is symbolic of the temporary huts that the Jews carried with them as they wandered the desert with Moses. Caution to non-Jews who have not mastered the Jewish "u" sound: this "u" is pronounced as the "u" in "put" or the "oo" sound in "foot"—not as the "u" in "sucka."

Sukkot (soo-COTE) The fall harvest festival that commemorates the Exodus out of Egypt by Moses and the Israelites and that expresses gratitude for the blessings of the earth.

synagogue (SIN-a-gog) The English word for the Jewish place of worship. It is also known as "temple" or the Yiddish *shul* (SHOOL).

temple Another English word for the Jewish place of worship.

tallit (tah-LEET) A prayer shawl worn by Jews in a place of worship.

Torah (TOE-rah) The first five books of the Bible: Genesis, Exodus, Leviticus, Numbers, and Deuteronomy. Many use this word as an abbreviation for *sefer Torah*. This refers to the scroll in a synagogue, which contains this history of the Jewish people.

Tribe, member of the An expression for "member of the Jewish people." It originates from the twelve tribes of Israel, descended from Jacob's twelve sons.

verklempt (ver-KLEMPT) Most famously used by Mike Myers of *Saturday Night Live* fame, this word has worked its way into the vocabulary of Jews and non-Jews alike. It basically means "choked up" or "about to cry." Myers, who is also in an interfaith marriage, would use this term while imitating his Jewish mother-in-law on the TV show. "I'm getting a little *verklempt*. Talk amongst yourselves."

yahrtzeit (YAHR-tsite) A Yiddish term referring to the anniversary of a loved one's death.

yarmulke (YAH-mi-kah) The Yiddish word for the skullcap worn as a sign of reverence. Some Jews wear them just in temple and at Jewish ceremonies. Some wear them everywhere. Some do not wear them at all. In Hebrew, it is called a *kippah* (KEE-pah). They are traditionally worn only by men, but today non-Orthodox women wear them as well.

FURTHER READING

Diamant, Anita. *The New Jewish Baby Book: Names, Ceremonies and Customs: A Guide for Today's Families*. 2nd ed. Woodstock, VT: Jewish Lights Publishing, 2005.

Eisenberg, Joyce, and Scolnic, Ellen. *The JPS Dictionary of Jewish Words*. Philadelphia: Jewish Publication Society, 2001.

Forman, Sharon. *Honest Answers to Your Child's Jewish Questions*. New York: URJ Press, 2006.

Gregory, David. *How's Your Faith? An Unlikely Spiritual Journey*. New York: Simon & Schuster, 2015.

Judson, Dan, and Nancy H. Wiener. *Meeting at the Well: A Jewish Spiritual Guide to Being Engaged*. New York: URJ Press, 2001.

Larkin, Jane. *From Generation to Generation: A Story of Intermarriage & Jewish Continuity*. Self-published, 2014.

Levin, Sunie. *Mingled Roots: A Guide for Grandparents of Interfaith Grandchildren*. New York: URJ Press, 2003.

McGinity, Keren R. *Marrying Out: Jewish Men, Intermarriage, and Fatherhood*. Bloomington: Indiana University Press, 2014.

McGinity, Keren R. *Still Jewish: A History of Women and Intermarriage in America*. New York: New York University Press, 2012.

Sweeney, Jon, and Rabbi Michal Woll. *Mixed-Up Love: Relationships, Family and Religious Identity in the 21st Century*. New York: Jericho Books, 2013.

Syme, Daniel B. *The Jewish Home: A Guide for Jewish Living*. Updated ed. Springfield, NJ: Behrman House, 2017.

Thompson, Jennifer A. *Jewish on Their Own Terms: How Intermarried Couples Are Changing American Judaism*. New Brunswick, NJ: Rutgers University Press, 2014.

ACKNOWLEDGMENTS

From the bottom of my heart, I would like to thank the following people: my parents and my wife's parents for their unending support, generosity, and love that made this book possible.

I would also like to thank Rabbi Hara Person of the former URJ Press, who originally helped to bring this book to fruition.

To all of the great people at Behrman House, including my editor, Aviva Gutnick, who polished and elevated *Inside Intermarriage* to a new level; executive editor Dena Neusner, who saw new opportunities for my book; designer Susan Neuhaus for a beautiful cover—I am forever grateful to all of you.

Special thanks to my readers, who made sure everything made sense: Jim Ball, Dr. Norman and Terry Cohen, Anita Diamant, Dru Greenwood, Kathy Kahn, and Joyce Schwartz.

I also would like to thank Ronnie Friedland, who expertly worked with me on the many articles I wrote for *InterfaithFamily*, where much of the material in this book originally appeared. In addition, I would be remiss if I didn't add that Edmund Case, founder of InterfaithFamily, created a much-needed resource for interfaith couples exploring Jewish life. Thanks for being on the forefront of this issue, Ed!

My gratitude also goes to the following people: Rabbi Bob Levy and the Reverend Dr. Bob Livingston, who welcomed my family "as is"; Dr. Jay Sandweiss for his direction and good jokes; and finally, the many other friends and family members who encouraged me or at least put up with me.

So many words of appreciation come to mind but just aren't worthy. Funny, I'm sure there's a Yiddish word for it.

ABOUT THE AUTHOR

Jim Keen has written for the *Detroit Jewish News, Atlanta Jewish Times, The Forward, Ann Arbor Family Press,* and *InterfaithFamily.* When not writing, Keen can be found traveling the country giving talks about interfaith marriage or chasing down students in his fifth grade classroom in the Ann Arbor Public Schools. He lives in Ann Arbor, Michigan, with his wife and two daughters.